VOICES IN THE STORM

VOICES

IN THE

STORM

Confederate Rhetoric, 1861–1865

Karen E. Fritz

UNIVERSITY OF NORTH TEXAS PRESS
DENTON, TEXAS

FIRST EDITION 1999
10 9 8 7 6 5 4 3 2 1

Permissions:
University of North Texas Press
PO Box 311336
Denton TX 76203-1336

The paper used in this book meets the minimum requirements
of the American National Standard for Permanence of Paper for Printed Library
Materials, z39.48.1984. Binding materials have been chosen for durability.

Library of Congress Cataloging-in-Publication Data
Fritz, Karen E., 1965–
Voices in the storm : Confederate rhetoric, 1861–1865 / Karen E. Fritz.
p. cm.
Includes bibliographical references (p.) and index.
ISBN 1-57441-077-6 (alk. paper)
1. Confederate States of America–Politics and government.
2. Confederate States of America–Social life and customs. 3. Political
oratory–Confederate States of America. 4. Rhetoric–Confederate
States of America. 5. Oratory–Confederate States of America.
6. Discourse analysis–Social aspects–Confederate States
of America. 7. United States–History–Civil War,
1861–1865–Social aspects. I. Title.
E487.F87   1999
815'.0109975'09034-dc21   99-20995
CIP

Book design and composition by Mark McGarry,
Texas Type & Book Works, Dallas, Texas

Set in Walbaum

To my parents

CONTENTS

ACKNOWLEDGMENTS

If I were to thank properly all the individuals who have assisted in the preparation of this document, these acknowledgments would run nearly as long as the book itself. I am especially indebted to Dr. Anne Loveland of Louisiana State University for her tireless work editing and helping to improve this manuscript. She held me to high standards and in so doing taught me a great deal about research and writing. I appreciate all of the guidance she has provided over the years. Dr. Stephen Hardin of The Victoria College deserves thanks for encouraging me towards publication and for his numerous and often humorous observations about writing, teaching, and practicing as a historian. I am also grateful to Mr. Charles Spurlin and Ms. Sandy Schramek, both of The Victoria College. Mr. Spurlin provided valuable assistance during publication, and Ms. Schramek typed and edited this document expertly and repeatedly and without complaint.

I am indebted to staffs at several libraries. In the course of my research I paid extensive visits to the Mississippi Department of Archives and History, the Archives and Manuscript Department at the Auburn University Library, Hill Memorial Library at Louisiana State University, the Center for American History at the University of Texas at Austin, and the South Caroliniana Library in Columbia. Librarians and archivists at each location proved helpful and friendly, and I greatly appreciate their patience and assistance. The inter-library loan staff at the Troy H. Middleton Library of Louisiana State University also rendered important service by quickly processing my many requests for documents and microfilm.

Several other individuals deserve mention as well. Susan Knisely, an excellent librarian, assisted me with computer database research. Rolene and Tommy Wall deserve thanks for their support and friendship during the preparation of this document. Dr. Henry Robertson of Louisiana State University assisted with the title. Dr. Melissa Wiedenfeld provided me with research opportunities that taught me a great deal about the practice of history. Thanks also to the editors and staff at the University of North Texas Press for their generous assistance with this work.

Finally, I acknowledge my parents, Thomas and Carol Fritz. I am quite aware that their generosity made my education possible. When I went away to college, they provided everything I needed. When I went to graduate school, they offered encouragement and support. And when I accepted my doctorate, they traveled hundreds of miles to cheer. They sacrificed a great deal so that I could pursue my dreams, and for that I thank them.

"The flow of Confederate history," observed Richard Harwell, "has never ceased." "First," he wrote, "it was motivated by desire for vindication. Soon every Confederate general was easily convinced that it would be a dereliction of his duty should he deny the public his memoirs." And in the twentieth century, Harwell concluded, "Continued interest in the war has justified continued examination. . . . and has made the American Civil War the best documented of all wars."[1] Modern scholars of the Civil War and Confederacy grapple with thousands of works on the South, the North, and the conflict, enough, says Harwell, "to fill whole libraries."[2]

The Confederacy attracts attention, some argue, because its story is inherently dramatic. Between 1861 and 1865 white southerners experienced shattering calamities as they waged their unsuccessful struggle for independence. Many lost homes and family members. Others watched as the maelstrom gradually consumed their cities and fields, polluted their rivers, and destroyed their social order. By 1865, southerners who once prided themselves on their independence, strength, and honor were living in the grip of poverty and defeat, their lives encompassed by loss, destruction, and ruin. Their story is gripping and readily available in firsthand accounts.

This book joins a long line of monographs that seek to discover how events affected the southern ethos. And in many ways, it resembles earlier studies in its description of a society altered by conflict. The work, though, is unusual in one respect, for it departs from primary reliance on diaries, letters, and newspapers, and adopts a form of inquiry based on another type of source altogether. The information presented in this book has been gleaned largely from Confederate speeches.

Oratory played a fundamental role in the southern nation, and citizens described encountering it almost daily at military functions, before battle, in church, and even while lying in hospital beds or strolling on city streets. Historians, of course, have recognized the significance of oratory in the Confederacy, and have often incorporated speeches into their works. Drew Gilpin Faust included sermons, speeches, and lectures in *The Creation of Confederate Nationalism* and engaged in detailed rhetorical analysis in *Southern Stories: Slaveholders in Peace and War*. Likewise, George Rable considered more than fifty-six speeches and sermons in *The Confederate Republic: A Revolution Against Politics*, his recent examination of Confederate political culture. References to oratory appear in older works as well. *Rebel Religion*, for example, Herman Norton's brief but entertaining work from 1961, included an effective section on sermons. In his book, Norton discussed the interplay between speaker and audience, the lengths of orations, and the difficult conditions

Confederate soldiers would accept in order to hear preaching. Clearly, the evidence in these and other works suggests that Confederate oratory has not been ignored by the historical community.[3]

The Confederacy is uniquely suited for a study based solely on speeches, for this type of analysis poses certain restrictions on subject matter. Any study based on rhetorical scholarship not only has to involve a large number of speeches, but also must include some input from speech audiences. One needs, after all, to know something about the situation in which an oration was delivered and the reception it received in order to make a thorough analysis. The Confederacy provides ample numbers of orations, and this work takes advantage of an abundance of complete speeches printed in newspapers or released as published documents. Paraphrases and extracts have been largely, though not completely, ignored. Also, because Confederate citizens frequently commented on oratory or spoke out during speeches, audience behavior and response has been noted when possible.

Readers familiar with Confederate oratory may notice that some speeches have been excluded from the collection of sources. Readers will also find that the speeches become fewer in number as the war years elapse. Declining numbers of speeches has proven to be an unavoidable difficulty, for as the war deprived the South of supplies, territory, and men, and as it increasingly destroyed southern cities, speech publication, though not speech-making, apparently began to lapse. By far the greatest number of surviving speeches date from the first year of the war. It is in part to reduce the imbalance in Confederate oratory from 1861 to 1865 that several sermons from the war's early years have been excluded. Sermons, in fact, have been generally culled to prevent the analysis from becoming too reliant on or too biased towards one form of oratory.

The work is organized thematically. The first chapter examines oratory within the Confederacy, while the second introduces the readers to the methods of analysis employed within the body of the text. The remainder are devoted to rhetorical analysis itself. The third chapter examines certain peculiarities within Confederate oratory from 1861, while subsequent sections explore themes that stand out in the speeches themselves (the natural environment, the southern character, the North) or that have particular significance according to the historical community (slavery). Each unfolds chronologically in order to reveal how Confederate oratory responded to the changing environment of the Civil War. The cited quotations best illustrate the conclusions drawn from rhetorical analysis, and readers are encouraged to read the endnotes for additional information judged interesting but too distracting to be included in the main body of the text. The speakers quoted in this work are all male, for, as many historians and rhetoricians have acknowledged, antebellum and Civil War-era southern women rarely gave speeches. Therefore, the pronoun "he" appears occasionally in general references to speakers. Research located only one female speaker.

Speech analysis reveals that the Civil War had a revolutionary effect on the South. It forced white southerners to reconsider or even jettison cherished beliefs about themselves, their setting, and their slaves. Confederate orators began the war by outlining a detailed and idealized portrait of their nation and its people. During the conflict, however, they gradually altered the depiction, increasingly adding references to the grotesque and discordant. By the end of the war, speakers described their nation in savage terms, applying to it expressions and characteristics once reserved only for the North. Speech analysis thus suggests something rather arresting. It indicates that southerners, engulfed in turmoil of war, listened as orators gradually shaped them and their nation into rhetorical facsimiles of their enemy. This suggests that separation at some level effected reunion.

Notes

1 Richard B Harwell, ed. *The Confederate Reader: How the South Saw the War* (New York: Dover Publications, Inc., 1989), xxiv.
2 *Ibid.*, xxiv.
3 Drew Gilpin Faust, *The Creation of Confederate Nationalism: Ideology and Identity in the Civil War South*, Walter Lynwood Fleming Lectures in Southern History, 1987 (Baton Rouge and London: Louisiana State University Press, 1988); Drew Gilpin Faust, *Southern Stories: Slaveholders in Peace and War* (Columbia, MO and London: University of Missouri Press, 1992); George C Rable, *The Confederate Republic: A Revolution Against Politics*, Civil War America Series, Gary W. Gallagher, editor (Chapel Hill and London: The University of North Carolina Press, 1994); Herman Norton, *Rebel Religion: The Story of Confederate Chaplains* (St. Louis: The Bethany Press, 1961).

CHAPTER ONE

Oratory in the Confederacy

BATON ROUGE resembled many southern towns during those first weeks of 1861. Barely a month had passed since South Carolina left the union, and the Louisiana capital echoed with talk of secession. Day and night, voices rose from street corners, restaurants, and meetings halls as southerners debated difficult questions about their region's future. To Irish immigrant William Watson, the scene appeared chaotic. From his self-described position as an "outsider, having little or no direct interest on either side," Watson studied the situation, taking note of the arguments for and against secession. Baton Rouge citizens, he said, seemed divided and uncertain as to "how all this was going to end."[1]

But as Watson looked on, he noticed that one activity seemed able to penetrate the confusion and even to direct the energy and focus of the crowds. This was oratory, and he watched as it rapidly took over the mediums of debate. As soon as South Carolina

seceded, he said, "politicians began to appear about the cafés . . ."
Then came meetings "held with audiences drummed up from
every available source." Finally, as the vote neared, there occurred
a veritable explosion of rhetoric. The city, he said, became
swamped with "political orators with all the soul-stirring elo-
quence that political education and practice could produce." By
mid-January, Watson noted that speakers could be heard on
"every platform, every café" and in every "street-corner crowd."[2]

What Watson observed in Baton Rouge should come as no sur-
prise to modern historians, for most accept that public speaking
played a central role in nineteenth-century southern culture.
Historians and rhetoricians, in fact, typically characterize the
antebellum South as a wellspring of oratory. Rhetorician Waldo
Braden, as part of his extensive studies of antebellum discourse,
noted that southerners heard oratory frequently, in every setting
"from the cabin to the statehouse," and in forms as varied as "sto-
rytelling, courtroom pleading, revival preaching, and, of course,
electioneering."[3] Similarly, Bertram Wyatt-Brown called the South
"an oral society," in which "the scarcity of lending libraries, books,
and literary societies, [and] the low state of education" came to
invest spoken words with tremendous significance. "The opportunity," according to Wyatt-Brown, "to exchange . . . words or hear
them eloquently pronounced was deeply cherished" throughout
the antebellum South.[4]

When one examines the Confederacy from a purely rhetorical
standpoint, it becomes evident that the circumstances of the Civil
War actually caused the level of southern discourse to increase.
Some scholars of rhetoric argue that speeches play a responsive
role in society, that they come into existence, in the words of Lloyd
Bitzer, to address "a specific condition or situation which invites
utterance." Such a condition Bitzer calls an "exigence," or an
imperfection of some type "marked by urgency . . . a defect, an

obstacle, . . . a thing which is other than it should be."[5] The Civil War, with its battles, death, destruction, ceremonies, shortages, political changes, and acts of bravery, contained countless exigencies and thus generated countless opportunities for discourse.

And Confederates responded fervently. On the homefront, even as orators reprised their antebellum roles as the spokesmen for lecture societies, holidays, graduations, and elections, they also took on a variety of new engagements that, barring secession and war, would not have existed. In the Spring of 1861, for example, the creation of the Confederate government provided abundant opportunities for speakers to talk about the new system and its advantages. Accordingly, a number of politicians shared the experience of Howell Cobb. Cobb participated in the writing of the Confederate Constitution and, like many of the framers, traveled home upon its completion, when the provisional government removed from Montgomery, Alabama. The trip proved exhausting. Though he meant to hurry back to his native Georgia in order to raise a volunteer regiment, Cobb nonetheless stopped frequently to address roadside crowds. Between Alabama and Georgia, he said he orated "at every town on the road," standing on stairs and balconies, shouting news about the government and talking about the Confederacy's future until he damaged his voice. At one of his last stops, Cobb could only rasp a few words and excuse himself, explaining to the disappointed crowd "I have spoken enthusiastically . . . and am quite hoarse."[6]

Indeed, if civilian diaries, letters, and recollections, and the records of newspapers are perused for speech evidence, these sources suggest that orators responded to Civil War exigencies with incessant speechmaking. Speakers presided after battles, gave patriotic addresses in public theaters, bloviated at mass rallies, spoke at funerals, delivered special war-related seminars, or took tours in which they bolstered popular feeling and promoted their new country. Wartime conditions did not retard this activity; having to address troops or crowds in the open air, orators climbed onto whatever was available, making podiums out of wagons, boxes, or even train cars. They spoke amid shellfire and bombardment, before angry soldiers and through civilian unrest. When frantic Richmond citizens rioted for bread in April 1863, speakers faced the mob and talked it down. And Senator Williamson Oldham, fleeing Virginia in March–April 1865, encountered a fellow politician who was willing to remain in the path of advancing Union soldiers to keep a speaking engagement. When Oldham stopped in Lexington, North Carolina, northern forces were rumored to be so near he "trembled for the consequences." Still, he remembered, Senator Gustavus Henry elected to remain in the town to fulfill an "appointment to speak." Oldham recalled with pride that Henry "felt it to be his duty to do all that he could to rally the country."[7]

At times, exigency drove orators to extraordinary lengths, to superhuman efforts fraught with peril or, in the case of Louisiana Governor Henry Watkins Allen, great physical discomfort. Elected in November 1863, Allen was crippled and in pain from a battle injury received the previous year. Charging towards a federal cannon in the Battle of Baton Rouge, he was struck point blank by an artillery shell. The blow left his legs shattered and, a year later, he still could not move without assistance.

Immediately after the election, however, Allen decided that recent events necessitated his taking a speaking tour. The war had not been kind to his state. By late 1863, parts of Louisiana lay under the control of the enemy; its finances were in disarray and its citizens afraid, poor, and uncertain. Allen told friends and family that these circumstances compelled him to travel, "to arouse the people, and to see what he had to do." Despite his condition, he toured some 450 miles and stopped for fourteen engagements, thus sacrificing his own comfort for the obligations of the orator.[8]

Similarly, in January 1865, Lucius Q. C. Lamar, once a mathematics professor at the University of Mississippi, risked death in the service of oratory. Having been invited to address a combat regiment, he traveled to the front lines outside Richmond. There, he found an eager, if weary, audience gathered to listen even as they took small arms and artillery fire. It was an eerie scene. Lamar climbed onto a stump and spoke amid "flickering torchlights, the rattle of . . . musketry on the skirmish line, the heavy detonation of . . . constant artillery fire . . ." His words raised cheers, which attracted attention, and soon enemy bullets began passing near his head and striking the wood around his feet. Lamar flinched in the onslaught, "ducking his head to the right or the left," but continued to speak. Concluding unharmed, he remarked on his good fortune, stating that "those Yankees must have owl's eyes."[9]

In the military, speechmaking infused nearly every phase of service. Officers and men told of enlistments inspired by orations and of training sites subject to a constant procession of speakers. As soldiers learned to drill and march, politicians visited; military orators spoke at dress parades, and preachers provided sermons. Treated to local barbecues and parties, troops enjoyed food, dancing, and socializing along with an array of optimistic and encouraging orations.

In training, two ceremonies in particular involved impressive amounts of oratory: the flag ceremony and the departure for war. Of the two, the flag ceremony generally took more time and included more speeches, rooted as it was far back in the enlistment process. Confederate men often joined the army in local units of company strength. Custom dictated that when these units went into training, their community of origin provided them with a battle flag generally sewed with care by local women. Few, if any, Confederate companies went to war without receiving such a

5

banner and, upon its bestowal, in order to honor the flag and to express their thanks for the gift, troops often put on showy drills and parades, held dances and banquets, and invited speakers to address the occasion.

The experience of the Delta Rifles of West Baton Rouge Parish, Louisiana, illustrates the centrality of oratory in such a ceremony. On April 20, 1861, the Rifles received a banner from parish ladies in what a local paper called a "brilliant ceremony." Festivities started in the morning when the troops formed up near the Mississippi River ferry depot, joined by two companies from Baton Rouge. Dressed in full uniform and standing in straight ranks with "martial bearing," the units first drilled before a large, admiring crowd, then marched to a prearranged location where they were to receive their banner. Excitement grew as the troops demonstrated more maneuvers, then froze in precise formation. Shortly thereafter, according to a local paper, "Mr. C. Sidney Lobdell advanced to present the flag. . . . When all was ready, he . . . addressed the Rifles."[10]

Lobdell's speech was not lengthy, but it was only the first of three orations delivered that afternoon. He spoke of the "bravery," "honor," and "chivalry" of the soldiers, of their duties and the reasons for war, and then presented the flag to the company captain. The latter, in turn, spoke briefly on behalf of the soldiers and gave the flag to his color bearer. The color bearer, a corporal, added a few words on the duties of southern men to defend their country and promised to protect and honor the banner. Following the presentation, celebrations continued into the night, and by the "late hour" at which festivities concluded, six more speeches had taken place.[11]

Departure ceremonies, though slightly less ostentatious, also involved a fair amount of oratory. Coming at the end of training, when soldiers went off to war, this ritual typically involved high emotion, large crowds, and several speakers. In one case, the embarkation of an elite artillery unit in April, 1861, drew a crowd of over 2,000 and prompted an hour of speechmaking. This particular farewell, held for the Athens, Georgia, Troupe Artillery, began with a sermon at the Methodist Church, followed by a procession to the train depot. There, Chancellor Lipscomb of the University of Georgia made a farewell oration, and the company's captain, Marcellus Stanley, replied. The ceremony finally concluded with what a local paper called a "most touching prayer," after which the artillerymen boarded and left for camps and battlegrounds in Virginia.[12]

Mustering into the Confederate army generally involved a degree of trauma, for camp life involved substantial changes in lifestyle. Away from home and among thousands of strangers, men dealt with homesickness, deadly diseases, filth, and constant exposure to vices such as gambling or drinking. Daily life also involved orders and discipline, boring routines, and long periods of lethargy and idleness that led to depression and sickness.[13] However, despite the social changes involved in military service, one aspect of life remained unchanged; in the army, orators were nearly as constant a presence as they were in training or on the home front.

Indeed, some accounts actually suggest that the Confederate army was as devoted to rhetoric as it was to fighting. Captain Henry Chambers, a student who left Davidson College in 1861 for service in Virginia and North Carolina, wrote of hearing some forty sermons, several speeches, and even a few lectures during a two-year period.[14] Likewise, Lieutenant Richard Lewis, a South Carolinian serving in Virginia, frequently wrote about oratory in his letters home. Writing to his mother in July, 1861, he mentioned listening to a "few very stirring strains . . . very loudly applauded" after a dress parade in Leesburg. In early 1863, a speaker reprimanded his unit for drunkenness, while in June of that same year, General D. H. Hill delivered a "very stirring and eloquent address, complimenting the brigade very highly." A variety of people spoke before the Confederate armies; soldiers mentioned visits from politicians (including President Jefferson Davis) and generals, as well as from lesser officers, preachers, chaplains, and civilians. One historian states that groups of soldiers were known to stand in rain and snow in order to hear sermons.[15]

Oratory even accompanied soldiers into battle, and a fine illustration of the connection between speechmaking and fighting emerges in the experience of Mississippian Robert Moore. On October 20, 1861, Moore's Mississippi infantry regiment marched towards Union forces near Leesburg, anticipating a fight within hours. "Battle and Yankees near," he wrote in his diary, adding "we are not expecting a fight today but would not be surprised if something was done tomorrow."[16] Moore, however, also recorded something else, for in the anxious hours before the fight he had apparently found a diversion. "When we halted here," he said, "Gen Evans and Col Featherston made us a short speech. The Gen said if we would die here he would die with us." Moore ended up in a frontal assault against a twelve-pound Federal cannon, but emerged from the battlefield unscathed. Returning to his diary, he noted how the experience ended for him in exactly the same way it began. We "have had a great day," Moore wrote. "Speeches were made by nearly all of our officers. Colonel Evans first addressed us and after all the officers had given an account of themselves . . . Rev. V. K. Marshall of Vicksburg addressed us."[17]

Eyewitness accounts thus reveal that tremendous amounts of discourse accompanied the creation and development of the Confederate nation. And, if one shifts focus from speakers to audience, one finds that this oratory took place in an environment both rewarding and difficult. Civil War southerners provided their orators with a huge and enthusiastic assemblage of listeners. Fascinated by speeches and speechmaking and often reliant on the spoken word for entertainment, news, and social commentary, Confederates received orations eagerly, their zeal undiminished by the passage of time.

Mary Chesnut noticed this propensity in Richmond, Virginia, in 1861. Crowds, she said, roamed the city for two nights after the first Battle of Manassas, seeking out officials for their comments on the occasion. During the second night, she wrote that "the crowd came to get [President Jefferson] Davis to speak to them. They wanted to hear all about it again."[18] Likewise, in 1865 the *Richmond Enquirer* reported that thousands competed for space inside the city's African Church in order to listen to speeches in defiance of the North. Some two thousand, said the paper, had to remain outside, "growling . . . upon the disappointment."[19] Soldiers also sought after oratory, their appetite for discourse unaffected by their military fortunes. Arriving in New Orleans after fighting in a severe and losing battle downriver at Fort Jackson, Captain William Seymour noted with pleasure that two speakers were present when he reported to the mayor.[20]

But enthusiasm did not always translate into amicability, for the same audiences that flocked to listen could also turn antagonistic. Southerners were known to heckle, to shout personal opinions or to demand words on specific subjects. They sometimes peppered speakers with questions or demands, constantly interrupted to applaud or cheer, or even drowned out some orators entirely. Most unnervingly, though, Southerners studied their speakers in great detail, taking note of every nuance, every flaw, every bit of awkwardness, and cataloguing dress and bearing so thoroughly that even objects held in a hand might not escape scrutiny.

9

Few orators escaped harassment or inspection, even well-respected, popular figures. In 1861, Alexander Stephens was beloved and honored in his native Georgia, but even so, before he could deliver his now famous "Cornerstone" speech in Savannah, he first had to order rowdy elements in the audience to quiet down.[21] War heroes also came under scrutiny. When General Stephen Lee addressed soldiers in the Army of Tennessee in late 1864, his lengthy service record, which dated back to Fort Sumter, did not shield him from audience critique. He spoke, according to one report, "very plainly" during an attempt "to get up a better feeling in his corps."[22]

The Confederate audience also read oratory as eagerly as it listened. Kate Cumming, an Alabamian who served as a military nurse, recalled how she and others so hungered for discourse during the secession crises that they pursued both written and spoken words with equal vigor. Looking back from 1895, she pointedly recalled, "We read with avidity the political speeches made North and South, and commented unsparingly upon their merits."[23] And private Benjamin Freeman indicated that even extreme reversal could not dampen the enthusiasm for written discourse. In March, 1865, Freeman wrote his wife a gloomy letter from the ruin around Petersburg, Virginia. Freeman was maimed; one of his arms hung "crooked" and useless from a recent wound, and all about he felt growing depression in the ranks. Still, amid the carnage of the siege of Petersburg, he had kept up with Confederate oratory well enough to request an account of a speech planned by North Carolina Governor Zebulon Vance. "I herd the other day," he wrote, ". . . that [he] was to make a speech in Louisburg if he do[es] I want you to write in your next letter what sort of speech it was."[24]

Freeman's request was not unusual, for, when denied the opportunity to witness an oration personally, many citizens sought a printed rendition. Speakers, clearly understanding their patrons, willingly provided texts upon request and benefited from newspapers, which devoted substantial amounts of copy to snippets, paraphrases, and orations in their entirety. The contents of newspapers, in fact, tell of a high demand for printed discourse; between January, 1861, and January, 1865, for example, the *Hillsborough Recorder* of Hillsborough, North Carolina printed all or parts of some thirty-four speeches, some of them quite lengthy. Included were the words of northern politicians, a number of sermons, a graduation address, and one speech from the ancient Roman empire. Papers from larger cities carried an even greater number of speeches. The *Charleston Daily Courier*, from April 11 to July 6, 1861, ran thirteen selections, an average of one per week. Even in Bellville, Texas, the *Bellville Countryman* carried speeches of northerners, generals, politicians, and foreigners.

In Confederate society, therefore, verbal discourse had a presence extending far beyond its spoken manifestation. Behind the crowds, the rallies, the cheers, and heckles, it also circulated quietly in written form, passing through the hands and capturing the attention of thousands of readers. Indeed, so thoroughly did oratory permeate Confederate society, that it became a means of common cultural expression, a medium through which southerners interpreted their surroundings and described their fellow citizens.

Several illustrations reveal the depth to which discourse informed culture. Speeches provided, for example, a means for evaluating the ability and character of those in power. In keeping with this function, some of the South's harshest criticisms of Abraham Lincoln stemmed from unfavorable evaluations of his speaking ability. An Alabama politician suggested in 1861 that southerners "compare the speeches of the President of these Confederate States with those of the President of the United States to feel proud of the contrast between the statesman and the narrow-minded and ignorant partisan."[25] Likewise, when Jefferson

Davis fell out of favor with certain members of his Congress in 1864, one attacked his oratorical capability. Rising in the Confederate House of Representatives, noted Davis enemy Henry Foote of Tennessee chose to express his disdain for the President in part by calling a recent Davis effort one of the "most disgusting specimen[s] of fustian and billingsgate oratory that has ever been uttered outside of an insane asylum."[26]

When writing about the people and events around them, southerners repeatedly used oratory as a means of description. Discussing the people he encountered while fighting in New Mexico in 1862, enlisted man A. B. Peticolas frequently represented them through their characteristics of speech. John Schmidt, Peticolas said, was "the oracle of his mess" and "talk[ed] incessantly." Philip Meyer, "another character," was "free of speech and . . . quite interesting," while Colonel Christopher "Kit" Carson was a "low, square-set, old plain farmer-looking man with a slow, quiet speech . . ."[27]

The tendency to describe and understand others through speech characteristics affected men and women, upper and lower classes alike. Pauline DeCaradeuc Heyward used speechmaking as a means to illustrate her brother's popularity in the army. "Mrs. H. said that the men all *loved* Tonio so much," she wrote, ". . . whenever any speech, or writing was to be made or done, they all wished him . . ."[28] Virginia Clay, wife of a wealthy Confederate senator, called her husband Clement a "great orator on paper as well as in speech" as a means of accentuating her feelings in a tender letter.[29] And James Nisbet, an educated young officer, in trying to compliment a fellow soldier, noted that he was "tall and handsome. He was a brilliant orator but without military education. By nature, he was a commander among men."[30]

Speech references even appeared in regard to subjects that themselves had little to do with oratory. In Confederate language, speeches became metaphors for a variety of activities including idolatry and warfare. Mary Chesnut described a woman's hero-worship of General Joseph Johnson as a "stump speech, if ever there was a stump speech."[31] Richard McCalla, an engineer on railroad projects in North Carolina and Tennessee, wrote his wife in 1864 that "The Yankees run like deer before the hounds." "Our soldiers are speaking out in trumpet tones to northern vandals. They will fight to the bitter end rather than be subjugated."[32]

One speaker even assigned oratory a central role in the southern war effort. During an 1863 sermon, the Reverend Stephen Elliott argued that Confederate citizens had lost some of the energy and enthusiasm they exhibited in 1861. He indicated that southerners could not "rekindle the sacred fire of patriotism" without oratory. "Where is the orator?" he asked. "Where are the voices, which, like a trumpet's blast, led on the soldier to the field of glory. . . ? They are all mute. . . . Where is the low sweet voice of woman which has mingled so harmoniously thro' all this tumult with the clangor of the trumpet and the clash of arms? Why is it unheard?" Elliott even went so far as to claim that God Himself recognized the importance and value of verbal discourse. In the Old Testament, he pointed out, as Moses led the Israelites from Egypt, God ordered him to "speak unto the children of Israel that they go forward."[33]

Confederates indicate that oratory played a significant role in the wartime South. Speechmaking was a constant; it garnished major events and provided Civil War southerners with a common means and terminology for evaluating and describing themselves, their leaders and friends, and their experiences. Speeches, therefore, potentially offer the historian a wealth of information. However, to unlock the data within Confederate discourse, one must first know something about the techniques of rhetorical analysis.

Notes

1 William Watson, *Life in the Confederate Army: Being the Observations and Experiences of an Alien in the South During the American Civil War* (London: Chapman & Hall, 1887; reprint, Baton Rouge and London: Louisiana State University Press, 1995), xv, 74.

2 *Ibid.*, 71.

3 Waldo W. Braden, *The Oral Tradition in the South* (Baton Rouge and London: Louisiana State University Press, 1983), ix.

4 Bertram Wyatt-Brown, *Southern Honor: Ethics and Behavior in the Old South* (New York and Oxford: Oxford University Press, 1982), 330.

5 Lloyd F. Bitzer, "The Rhetorical Situation," *Philosophy and Rhetoric* 1(1968): 4, 6.

6 Howell Cobb, Speech at Atlanta, Georgia, delivered May 22, 1861, in *Echoes from the South Comprising the Most Important Speeches, Proclamations, and Public Acts Emanating from the South during the Late War* (New York: E. B. Treat & Co., 1866), 187.

7 For mention of a speech delivered from atop a train see Kate Cumming, *Kate: The Journal of a Confederate Nurse*, ed. Richard Barksdale Harwell (Baton Rouge: Louisiana State University Press, 1959), 160. For mention of a sermon delivered under shellfire, see James B. Sheeran, *Confederate Chaplain: A War Journal of Rev. James B. Sheeran, C.SS.R 14th Louisiana, C.S.A.*, ed. Joseph T. Durkin, S. J., with a Preface by Bruce Catton (Milwaukee: The Bruce Publishing Co., 1960), 71–72. Williamson Simpson Oldham, "Last Days of the Confederacy," 1869, typed manuscript, The Center for American History, The University of Texas Austin, 3–5.

8 Sarah A. Dorsey, *Recollections of Henry Watkins Allen, Brigadier-General Confederate States Army, Ex-Governor of Louisiana* (New York: M Doolady, 1866), 238. The account of Allen's wounding can be found on page 138. Details of the inauguration are on 235–39. Information about the number of engagements on Allen's tour from Vincent H. Cassidy and Amos E. Simpson, *Henry Watkins Allen of Louisiana* (Baton Rouge: Louisiana State University Press, 1964), 178.

9 Edward Mayes, *Lucius Q C. Lamar: His Life, Times, and Speeches, 1825–1893*, 2d ed. (Nashville: Publishing House of the Methodist Episcopal Church South, Barbee & Smith Agents, 1896), 115.

10 C. Sidney Lobdell, Speech at the Flag Presentation to the Delta Rifles, Baton Rouge, Louisiana, delivered April 20, 1861, in *West Baton Rouge Sugar Planter*, April 27, 1861.

11 *Ibid.*

12 Kenneth Coleman, *Confederate Athens* (Athens: University of Georgia Press, 1967), 35–36.

13 For a treatment of camp life boredom, see Gerald F. Linderman, *Embattled Courage: The Experience of Combat in the American Civil War* (New York: The Free Press, A Division of MacMillan, Inc., 1987), 119.

14 Henry A. Chambers, *Diary of Captain Henry A. Chambers*, ed. T. H. Pearce (Wendell, NC: Broadfoot's Bookmark, 1983).

15 Richard Lewis, *Camp Life of a Confederate Boy, of Bratton's Brigade, Longstreet's Corps, C.S.A.: Letters Written by Lieut. Richard Lewis, of Walker's Regiment, to his Mother, during the War: Facts and Inspirations of Camp Life, Marches, Etc.* (Charleston: The News and Courier Book Presses, 1883; reprint, Garthersburg, MD: The Butternut Press, n. d.), 11, 38, 51; Herman Norton, *Rebel Religion: The Story of Confederate Chaplains* (St. Louis: The Bethany Press, 1961), 70.

16 Robert Moore Diary, October 20, 1861, Manuscript, Mississippi Department of Archives and History, Jackson, Mississippi.

17 *Ibid.*, October 24, 1861.

18 C. Vann Woodward, ed., *Mary Chesnut's Civil War* (New Haven and London: Yale University Press, 1981), 112.

19 *Richmond Enquirer*, February 10, 1865.

20 William J. Seymour, *The Civil War Memoirs of Captain William J. Seymour: Reminiscences of a Louisiana Tiger*, ed. Terry L. Jones (Baton Rouge and London: Louisiana State University Press, 1991), 37.

21 Alexander Stephens, Speech delivered in Savannah, Georgia, March 21, 1861, known as "The Corner Stone Speech," reported in the *Savannah Republican*, in Henry Cleveland, *Alexander Stephens, in Public and in Private, with Letters and Speeches before, during, and since the War* (Philadelphia: National Publishing Co., 1866), 718. Historians usually refer to this speech using one word: "Cornerstone," and I have used it that way in the text. In the source, however, it is listed as "Corner Stone," and I have left it that way in the source and the notes. What Stephens warned was, "I cannot

speak so long as there is any noise or confusion. I shall take my time—I feel quite prepared to spend the night with you if necessary."

22 Hubert Dent to wife, September 7, 1864, Letters in Dent Confederate Collection, Archives and Manuscripts Department, Auburn University Library, Auburn, Alabama.

23 Kate Cumming, *Kate: The Journal of a Confederate Nurse*, ed. Richard B. Harwell (Baton Rouge: Louisiana State University Press, 1959), xi, quoting Kate Cumming, *Gleanings from Southland* (Birmingham: 1895), 19.

24 Benjamin H. Freeman, *The Confederate Letters of Benjamin H. Freeman*, comp. and ed. Stuart T. Wright (Hicksville, NY: Exposition Press, 1974), 62.

25 Robert H. Smith, *An Address to the Citizens of Alabama, on the Constitution and Laws of the Confederate States of America by the Hon. Robert H. Smith, at Temperance Hall, on the 30th of March, 1861* (Mobile: M*obile Daily Register Print*, 1861), 6.

26 Henry Foote, Remarks on his resolution, delivered in the Confederate House of Representatives, November 9, 1864, paraphrased in "Proceedings of the Second Confederate Congress . . ." *Southern Historical Society Papers*, vol. 51, ed. Frank E. Vandiver (Richmond: The Virginia Historical Society, 1958; reprint, Broadfoot Publishing Company, 1992), 286–87.

27 A. B. Peticolas, *Rebels on the Rio Grande: The Civil War Journal of A. B. Peticolas*, ed. Don E. Alberts (Albuquerque: University of New Mexico Press, 1984), 134, 136, 120.

28 Pauline DeCaradeuc Heyward, *A Confederate Lady Comes of Age: The Journal of Pauline DeCaradeuc Heyward, 1863–1888*, ed. Mary D. Robertson (Columbia: University of South Carolina Press, 1992), 39.

29 Bell Irvin Wiley, *Confederate Women*, Contributions in American History, No. 38 (Westport, CN and London: Greenwood Press, 1975), 58.

30 James Cooper Nisbet, *Four Years on the Firing Line*, ed. Bell Irvin Wiley (Jackson, TN: McCowat-Mercer Press, Inc., 1963; reprint, Wilmington, NC: Broadfoot's Publishing Co., 1987), 7. The fellow southerner was John B. Gordon, then in his late twenties.

31 Woodward, *Mary Chesnut's Civil War*, 700.

32 Richard McCalla to wife, March 10, 1864, Speake–McCalla Civil War Correspondence, Archives and Manuscript Department, Auburn University, Auburn, Alabama.

33 Stephen Elliott, *Ezra's Dilemma. A Sermon Preached in Christ Church, Savannah, on Friday, August 21, 1863, Being the Day of Humiliation, Fasting and Prayer, Appointed by the President of the Confederate States, by the Rt. Rev. Stephen Elliott, D. D., Rector of Christ Church, and the Bishop of the Diocese of Georgia* (Savannah, GA: Power Press of George N. Nichols, 1863), 23–24.

CHAPTER TWO

Analyzing Confederate Rhetoric: Insights into Southern Oratory

SPEECH ANALYSIS may offer a fresh approach to history, but the historian who adopts this method soon learns it is difficult to implement. Deficiencies in available source materials often hamper analysis; in the Confederacy, though many speeches survive, they constitute only a fraction of the orations delivered from 1861 to 1865. Furthermore, the collection that remains is weighted in favor of the first two years of the Civil War. Few election or campaign speeches survive, and some complete orations have limited value due to gaps or inaccuracies in their content. Speakers, after all, recognizing that their orations frequently circulated in written form, sometimes altered wording and content between delivery and printing, and eyewitness reports may have misconstrued or misrepresented a speaker's words.

Speech analysis also involves some technical considerations; rhetoricians have developed a number of theories about their field and a number of different approaches to oratorical analysis. To extract cultural and social information from a speech, the historian must learn and understand the principles of discourse and choose a suitable method of examination from the many possibilities available.

Like historians, rhetoricians often disagree about their scholarship and frequently revise each other. However, they recognize certain basic principles of discourse. Of significance to this study is the presumption that speeches are persuasive devices. Rhetoricians generally agree that when an orator interacts with an audience, his speech serves as a means of influence, as the instrument through which he unveils his ideas, arguments, plans of action, and through which he urges the audience to accept his thoughts. This premise does not change in regard to subject matter; scholars have identified influential elements not only in campaign speeches and political discourse, but also in less coercive forms of oratory, including funeral and ceremonial addresses. Much of rhetorical analysis, therefore, involves examination of the art of persuasion.

But if scholars agree about the influential nature of oratory, they disagree over the specific factors that shape the persuasive effort and over the methods employed by the speaker. This work, as it seeks a blending of rhetorical and historical scholarship, holds to theories put forward by rhetoricians Ernest Bormann and Lloyd Bitzer. Writing in the 1960s and early 1970s, both men dealt with the relationship between oratory and society and concluded that the contents of a speech are greatly affected by the cultural and social traditions surrounding its delivery. Bormann, concerned with the interaction between speaker and audience, challenged scholars who dismissed the value of spoken words as sources for cultural analysis. Public speaking, he wrote, like all forms of human communication, involves an attempt to create a common identity within a group of people. The orator may test various beliefs, attitudes, and values as he seeks to connect with the listeners, but he will not purposefully create "dissonance." In other words, the words of a successful speaker do not challenge or come from outside the social context of the audience. Instead, according to Bormann, they "*are the social context.*"[1]

Lloyd Bitzer, writing about the circumstances that generate rhetorical discourse, agreed with Bormann on several points. Bitzer argued that a speech, in order to be persuasive, must fit the situation in which it is delivered. In part, that means it must provide an appropriate response to whatever occurrence is being addressed. But also, and of significance to the application of rhetoric to history, it must interact properly with the audience, taking into account their "sources of constraint," including "beliefs, attitudes, . . . traditions, images, interests, motives, and the like."[2] A speech which incorrectly responds to occasion, audience, and constraints, or one in which one of these areas is flawed, will fail to convey its message.

The arguments of Bormann and Bitzer suit Confederate study because they agree with what historians know about nineteenth-century southern oratory. Southern speakers, frequently students of rhetorical theory, were minutely aware of the importance of both audience and situation in speechmaking. Some altered their wording, expressions, and even their dress in order, as Bitzer might say, to fit the surrounding environment. They even used a colloquial expression to describe how connections were established between themselves and their listeners. Itinerate orators talked openly and sometimes boastfully about "going down to the people," the practice of pre-speech handshaking and mingling with members of the audience in order to learn their dialect, beliefs, and values. Bormann and Bitzer have applied technical terms to behavior that southerners practiced both before and during the Civil War.

Unlocking the social and cultural information within a speech requires rhetorical analysis on several levels. Such examination can be a highly esoteric and theoretical activity, but this study adopted fairly simple methods. Speeches were examined in chronological order and reduced to their argumentative and stylistic devices. In oratory, every rhetorical method or device has a different function as well as a unique set of advantages and limitations. Studying their use provided insight into how speakers approached their audiences, internalized their surroundings, and conceptualized their arguments.

This type of analysis did not, however, capture the totality of the experience, for written accounts fail to convey the elements of delivery: the speaker's tone of voice, subtle nuances, gestures, and overall presence. This presented something of an analytical quandary, for though all techniques of argument are ultimately transmitted through delivery, this facet of public speaking, in the words of rhetorician Halford Ryan, is "fleeting by its very nature," and "extremely difficult to sound."[3] With Confederate rhetoric, it is not possible to create a precise aural record. Periods of emotional or powerful delivery, however, do emerge through audience reactions or in the punctuation marks included by transcribers.

Eyewitness observations were also used to reach some general conclusions about behavior and style. It is known, for example, that Robert Toombs of Georgia was consistently described as a powerful speaker. Lucius Q. C. Lamar received praise in 1864 for speaking in "flowing sentences . . . well calculated to send his hearers home happy." Henry Foote, it was said, had a "hot temper and personal courage" and spoke in a manner "untiring and vitriolic."[4] Though these methods do not produce a thorough portrait of every speech, they help to enlighten a scholar as to what actually happened when a Confederate orator stood before an audience.

Technical analysis, however, remains the central focus of this work. And though not intended as an end unto itself, this method of inquiry produced some intriguing insights into the overall nature of Confederate discourse, insights which in turn raised questions about how historians have characterized southern oratory. Historically, the activity has been described as dramatic, flamboyant, and marked by excessive gesturing and verbosity. In 1943, Merle Curti wrote that yeomen enjoyed "the flowery oratory at the hustings," and that planters adopted an "embroidered oratorical rhetoric . . . as ephemeral as it was florid."[5] William J. Cash asserted that the Civil War infused southern politics with "that final term of southern extravagance, that significant type of people's captain, the fire-eating orator and mob master." This individual, Cash said, "gave the masses gasconade and bluster. . . ."[6] If historians are correct, one might expect the Confederacy, given the dramatic events surrounding its lifespan, to feature nothing but florid, grandiose oratory, oratory based largely on techniques designed to manipulate the emotions.

But it did not. Technical examination indicates that Confederate speakers were not wedded solely to grandiloquence. In general, speakers employ one of three strategies of persuasion. They may confront the emotions, relying on vivid descriptions and florid language to arouse feeling in the listeners. An ethical appeal might be selected, allowing the speaker to approach the audience person-to-person, seeking to sway by portraying himself as a man of good character. Or, an orator might choose an appeal to reason. Each strategy affects the overall tone of a speech, for obviously an oration based largely on appeals to the emotions will sound very different from one that is founded on reason and logic.

In Confederate oratory, no single approach completely dominated, and many orations contained mixtures of the three. A few examples illustrate the range of appeals. In January, 1865, Texan Williamson Oldham spoke before the Senate in a vain attempt to rekindle the South's fighting spirit. He chose to accost the emotions with dramatic language, at one point invoking a string of grotesque images, a series of exaggerated pictures of the wreckage of war:

> Can we forget our slaughtered sons, brothers, and countrymen? Can the father forget his murdered boy; and will not the mangled form, the mutilated limb of the remaining one be ever before him? Can the widow, "with all her household gods [sic] shattered around her," and her helpless and unprotected orphans, cease to mourn their murdered husband and father? Can the affectionate mother ever become deaf to the plaintive moans of her once pure and intellectual, but now violated maniac daughter? . . . Can that gulf between the North and the South, dug by hostile bayonets, wide and deep, extending from the ocean to the mountains of the west, filled with the reeking blood of our slain martyrs, from which the wailings of our people ever issue forth, and over which the fires of our burning homes are ever blazing, be closed and forever obscured. . . ? We can but die! Better to die ten thousand deaths than to live in such a union, of wrong, of hate, of scorn, of shame, of infamy, and degradation![7]

For this occasion, Oldham spoke vividly and dramatically about the war and its consequences. But Confederate orators did not always echo his dramatic tone. Alongside examples of grandiloquence, there were also studies in calm, methodical delivery, appeals lightened with humor, and serious orations emphasizing reason rather than emotion. Furthermore, subject matter did not determine the tone of appeal. In November, 1864, just a few months before Oldham delivered his address, another Confederate Congressman also attempted to raise morale, this time as part of a speech against drafting slaves into military service. Arguing that the South was fully capable of defending itself without black assistance, Henry Chambers of Mississippi spoke calmly and smoothly, citing statistics about the army and appealing to reason and logic:

> In 1862 there were 700,000 men between the ages of 18 and 45, in the cotton States, and over half a million more in Virginia, North Carolina and Tennessee. With a large allowance for physical disability, exemptions and details, here were about one million of men liable to field service under the acts of conscription, exclusive of all recruits from Kentucky and Missouri. Allowing one-fifth of the whole to be now within the enemy's lines, there would still remain 800,000 men; and if one half of this number have been lost or disabled in service, (*which is impossible*), there would still remain 400,000, a force more than sufficient to end this war soon and successfully, to say nothing of the Confederate Reserves and the Militia in the several States.[8]

Segments phrased for the ethical appeal also offer evidence contradictory to the historical interpretation of southern oratory. This type of appeal often appears in the beginning of a speech and usually contains generous use of the first person. It also involves careful attention to wording and expression, for, as it is the speaker's own person and character that is discussed, his offending or confusing the audience risks their alienation. Therefore, if Confederate orators believed audiences consistently expected flamboyance and drama, they would have shaped all ethical sections accordingly. An analyst might then expect every such appeal to sound the same.

However, the level of drama, intensity, and flowery language in ethical appeals varied greatly from speech to speech, and speaker to speaker. Sometimes orators shouted up their own abilities in exaggerated language. On other occasions, they connected with the audience quietly and serenely. Speaking about himself in a speech about the South's new Constitution in March, 1861, Robert Smith delivered a fine example of an ethical appeal that did not exaggerate his abilities or sound dramatic. Toning down his approach, Smith presented himself as a common, unremarkable individual:

> I have . . . invited your attendance this evening to lay before you, so far as an observance of the secrecy of our proceedings will admit, the course and action of the Congress of the Confederate States of America and to express my views of the destiny of our New Republic. I shall seek to discharge the task plainly and simply; for my object is not to entertain you with a speech, but to converse with you as a neighbor.[9]

That Confederate oratory cannot be characterized exclusively becomes even more apparent when one examines how speakers employed individual devices of argument and style. All speeches are collections of specific forms of argument, figures of speech, stories, and planned digressions through which the speaker establishes the tone of his discourse and develops his ideas and arguments. As each element functions differently, to understand fully the contents of an oration, one must study their deployment and use. Determining, for example, when a speaker chose a particularly strong means of persuasion can reveal much about his confidence in his subject, and about what he thought was most important to convey.

In Confederate speeches, this examination confirmed the multidimensional nature of southern oratory, for in their use of the basic methods of argument and style, Confederate speakers assumed a variety of different lexicons. Arguing from devices of argument like precedent and expert testimony, Congressmen and preachers sounded like lawyers. Using definition to discuss the role and designs of God, politicians adopted the wording and lofty expressions of ministers. And sometimes, especially through the use of stylistic elements such as hyperbole and metaphor, orators were flamboyant, grandiose, and pompous.

Again, several examples illustrate speakers' versatility. First, an 1861 oration by Alexander Stephens illustrates a deliberate effort from a man often described as a charismatic orator. Discussing the need for cotton planters to invest in the Confederacy, Stephens did not speak furiously or attempt to charm, but supported his arguments through less pretentious means. He drew comparisons, he spoke syllogistically, and he cited statistics, assuming at various points the dry language of a banker or economist:

> Can we cope with the North?–that is the question. We have not less than four thousand millions of taxable property within the Confederate States upon the last minimum estimate. At last year's rates, we therefore could raise from one hundred millions to two hundred millions, for years to come and yet survive. The wealth of nations, the ability of nations to sustain war, depends not so much upon its taxable property as its productive capital. It is to the latter we must look for the means and ability to sustain war, for in times of war generally all business is interrupted. . . . No nation in the world with the same population, has such a continuous annual productive capital.[10]

Other speakers made use of more compelling devices of persuasion, but not always to the same effect. For example, repetition is a key factor in many rhetorical devices, for the systematic recurrence of a single word, series of words, or even an individual sound generally stirs some type of reaction. Though repetition techniques can be and often are made to address the emotions, Confederate orators used these devices for a variety of purposes. Politician Henry Wise, discussing the character and techniques of the fighting man of 1861, inserted several different forms of repetition into his speech in order to add rhythm and additional energy to an already emotional discourse:

> Collect *yourselves*, summon *yourselves*, elevate *yourselves* to the high and sacred duty of patriotism. *The man who* dares to pray, *the man who* dares to wait until some magic arm is put into his hand; *the man who* will not go unless he have a Minié, or percussion musket, who will not be content with flint and steel . . . is worse than a coward—he is a renegade. . . . If their guns reach further than yours, reduce the distance; meet them *foot to foot, eye to eye, body to body*, and when you strike a blow, strike home.[11] [Emphasis added.]

On another occasion, though, Robert Smith used a particularly powerful type of repetition for a purpose more subtle than brash. In his speech at Mobile, Smith briefly turned to anaphora to describe one advantage of the South's new Constitution. Anaphora involves pattern repetition; in a series of statements, the orator will maintain the same grammatical structure for each and will begin each with the same word or group of words. When an analyst reads an oration, the recurrence of the same words in the same place again and again makes anaphora easy to identify. Of its use, one rhetorical scholar says that whenever it appears, "we can be sure that the author has used it deliberately. Since the repetition of the words helps to establish a marked rhythm . . . [it] is usually reserved for those passages where the author wants to produce a strong emotional effect."[12]

Smith's use of anaphora, though, illustrates that the device does not always have to assault the emotions. Attempting to teach the contents of the new Constitution, he employed anaphora simply to make an otherwise dry passage more catching:

> *By* refusing to a mere majority of Congress unlimited control over the treasury, and *by* requiring the yeas and nays to be taken when-

ever two-thirds assume to vote away money not asked for by the Executive; *by* placing upon the administration the duty and responsibility of calling for appropriations; *by* virtually excluding Congress from passing upon claims against the Government; *by* prohibiting extra compensation to employees; *by* enabling the Executive to be heard on the floor of Congress, and *by* giving the President the power to veto objectionable items in appropriation bills, we have, I trust, greatly purified our Government, and, at the same time, placed its different parts in nearer and more harmonious relations.[13] [Emphasis added.]

Revising the notion that southern oratory always involved drama and flamboyance does not require examples from every device adopted by Confederate speakers. Indeed, such a thorough treatment would change the purpose of this work. Technical analysis contributes to the interpretation of Confederate society by revealing a level of seriousness in the culture. That orators did not always speak dramatically suggests that southern audiences regularly wanted to hear more than entertaining grandiosity or bombast.

If speeches are to uncover a more complete social and cultural portrait of the Confederacy, however, the analytical perspective must expand to encompass not only how arguments were formatted, but also to address what was said and why. The speaker's choice of words and his use of metaphor, colloquialisms, and descriptions must come under scrutiny. Subjects developed through strong techniques need to be differentiated from those that were not. The analyst should also identify the objects and behaviors condemned in a speech, those defined as desirable or good, the consequences threatened, and the objects compared. For this work, this expanded type of examination has been labeled content analysis.

It is when technical and content analysis combine that a full account of the cultural and social constraints mentioned by Bitzer begins to emerge. An oration cited earlier may be used to illustrate the process. At one point in his 1865 discourse, Williamson Oldham urged citizens to follow the strength and example set by his home state:

> ... Texas is prepared "to take no step backwards"; ... she will do her whole duty and will share with her sister States any and every fate but that of submission and re-union; ... should any of the States, in an hour of adversity, desert the common cause, which pride, manhood, and honor forbid, or should all desert her, she will, single-handed, maintain the contest and continue "to tread the wine-press alone," and never cease it while there is an arm to strike a blow of resistance; never, until the bright, smiling prairie homes of her people shall be made desolate wastes, and her last son lie an immolated martyr upon her soil.[14]

Technical analysis of this short passage reveals it was designed to convey its message aggressively. First, Oldham placed it very near the beginning of the discourse, suggesting he wanted this point about strength and determination to stand out. Phrasing the section as an ethical appeal on behalf of Texas, Oldham tried to convince the audience of her good character and strength by exaggerating her devotion to the war effort. Texas, he said, would "single-handedly" keep fighting, and "never cease" until all her citizens were dead. This was hyperbole, a device that enhances the effect of the speaker's words so as to make them memorable.

Content analysis reveals the cultural identity reflected in this passage. Oldham equated the end of the war and re-union with "submission," a word suggesting lack of power and complete obedience, and then stated firmly that Texas would not accept this condition. Of the forces keeping the South in the fight, Oldham chose to name "pride, manhood, and honor" as the prime motivators, indeed as the factors that actually "forbade" any state from leaving the Confederacy. These words indicate that Oldham believed Confederates still valued and responded to the concept of honor even as their war effort failed, their armies weakened, and their morale crumbled. The passage also reveals a concern with nature; he chose to cite the destruction of natural beauty, the transformation of "bright, smiling prairie homes" into "desolate wastes," as a supreme sacrifice, choosing this over economic or material losses.

Speaking before the Confederate Congress, Oldham had to select words and themes that would appeal to people from across the South. His choices from an especially powerful section tell the analyst that he felt he could persuade southerners to keep fighting by convincing them that surrender would destroy their honor and manhood. In addition, that he included a passage about the destruction of natural beauty rather than a discussion of economic crises indicates where he believed the audience placed their concern. Of course, it is possible that Oldham's assessment is incorrect or, as one school or rhetorical theory might argue, merely a reflection of his own interpretation of the South. Analysis carried to its fullest extent would test his words by comparing them to the contents of contemporary speeches and by studying the popular reception given this oration.

Cultural insights can also be gained from what the speaker does not say. Henry Chambers, in his 1864 speech against arming slaves, had this, among things, to say about black soldiers:

> . . . if, as our despairing friends declare, we have approximated to final exhaustion, and must find some extraordinary source of reinforcements—will negro [sic] troops answer the purpose—will the African save us? . . . In what form of organization is it proposed to

use them? It can hardly be designed to intermingle them in the same companies with our citizen soldiers; no one has yet had the audacity to propose that. Would it be safe to confide to negro troops so much of the line of battle as would be occupied by a regiment or a brigade–much less a division or a corps? . . . one alternative remains; it is to form them into companies and place these in alternation with white companies in the same regiments. The electric current of mutual confidence and devotion . . . no longer passes from company to company. The silence of distrust now broods along the line, which hesitates, halts, wavers, breaks, and the black troops fly–perhaps to the embraces of the enemy.[15]

Technically, this passage involved rhetorical questions and a type of probability argument. Rhetorical questioning provides one of the most effective means of influence, for it offers the orator a certain amount of control over the audience. When people hear a question, they tend to formulate some type of response. When a speaker knows how the audience is likely to respond, rhetorical questions can be used to persuade obliquely in place of a direct statement. In Chambers's case, he did not believe black soldiers could benefit the South, and his blunt, even sarcastic "Will the African save us?" indicates that he thought his audience did not believe this either. Had Chambers any doubt about their answer to the question, he would not have allowed them the freedom of response. Instead, he would have directly argued for his opinion.

Content analysis reveals that Chambers meant for this passage to convey a very high level of racist feeling. He called the suggestion that blacks serve in the army "extraordinary," differentiated them from the "citizen soldiers," and expressed horror at the "audaci[ous]" notion of blacks being "intermingle[d]" with whites. To close this section, Chambers turned to themes of slave runaways and slaves in rebellion. Claiming that black soldiers would destroy the "electric current of mutual confidence" among the troops, he described a mixed army that wavered and hesitated in battle. The lines, he said, halt, then break, and the "black troops fly, perhaps to the embraces of the enemy." Chambers did not flatly state that these troops would then turn back against their masters, but hinted as much through his last statement. Again, the oblique reference indicates he did not feel he had to explain this fear completely, but felt that his audience understood implicitly.

Most historians would agree with the cultural and social information gleaned from Oldham's and Chambers's speeches. Honor, racism, and the fear of slave rebellion were significant themes in the South before and during the war. The point of this work, though, is not to promote a new method for identifying the obvious. Rather, in order to gain insight into southern society, speech analysis is employed to identify the central themes of Confederate rhetoric, to analyze what these reveal about the Civil War South, and to determine the extent to which they were altered by the war. Paired with information gained from historical scholarship, this approach should offer insights about the extent to which four years of violent conflict and the experiences of secession and nation-building reshaped the mentality of the American South. The examination begins with the speeches of 1861, with the oratory delivered as southerners embarked on their struggle for independence.

Notes

1   Ernest G Bormann, "Fantasy and Rhetorical Vision: The Rhetorical Criticism of Social Reality," in *Quarterly Journal of Speech*, 58 (1972), 399, 400. On page 401, Bormann further states that an analyst should be able to "take the social reality contained in a rhetorical vision . . . and examine the social relationships, the motives, the qualitative impact of that symbolic world as though it were the substance of social reality for those people who participated in the vision."

2   Lloyd F. Bitzer, "The Rhetorical Situation," in *Philosophy and Rhetoric*, 1 (1988), 8.

3   Halford Ryan, ed., *U. S. Presidents as Orators: A Bio-Critical Sourcebook* (Westport, CN and London: Greenwood Press, 1995), xi.

4   William Y. Thompson, *Robert Toombs of Georgia*, The Southern Biography Series, ed. T. Harry Williams (Baton Rouge: Louisiana State University Press, 1966), 19, 109. Observers specifically remarked on Toombs's cogent and eloquent style of delivery. In 1839, he was described as "bold, fluent, sarcastic," . . . "clear in illustration . . . wholly indifferent to rhetorical embellishment." This was echoed in 1856 by Alexander Stephens's statement that Toombs was "the ablest debater and most eloquent man. . . . For originality of thought and power of expression he has no equal." Edward Mayes, *Lucius Q. C. Lamar: His Life, Times, and Speeches, 1825–1893*, 2d. ed. (Nashville: Publishing House of the Methodist Episcopal Church, South, Barbee and Smith, Agents, 1896), 114, quoting *Columbus Enquirer*, March 25, 1864; Mayes, 51.

5   Merle Curti, *The Growth of American Thought*, 3d ed. (New York and London: Harper & Row, Publishers, 1964), 424, 429

6   William J. Cash, *The Mind of the South* (New York: Alfred A. Knopf, 1941), 79.

7   Williamson Oldham, Speech of Hon. W. S. Oldham, of Texas, on the Resolutions of the State of Texas, Concerning Peace, Reconstruction, and Independence, delivered in the Confederate Senate on January 20, 1865 (n. p.), 12. The Center for American History, The University of Texas at Austin.

8   H[enry] C. Chambers, Policy of Employing Negro Troops. Speech of Hon. H. C. Chambers, of Mississippi, in the House of Representatives of the Congress of the Confederate States, Thursday, November 10, 1864, on the special order for that day, being the resolution offered by him on the first day of the session . . . (n. p., n. d.), 2.

9   Robert H. Smith, *An Address to the Citizens of Alabama on the Constitution and Laws of the Confederate States of America, by the Hon. Robert H. Smith, at Temperance Hall, on the 30th day of March,* 1861 (Mobile: Mobile Daily Register Print, 1861), 3.

10 Alexander Stephens, Speech at Augusta, Georgia, delivered July 11, 1861, in Frank Moore, ed, *The Rebellion Record: A Diary of*

American Events with Documents, Narratives, Illustrative Incidents, Poetry, Etc., vol. 2 (New York: D. Van Nostrand, 1866), 278.

11 Henry Wise, Speech in Springs, 1861, date unknown, location unknown [Richmond, June 1, 1861], in *Echoes from the South Comprising the Most Important Speeches, Proclamations, and Public Acts Emanating from the South during the Late War* (New York: E. B. Treat & Co., 1866), 152–53.

12 Edward P. J. Corbett, *Classical Rhetoric for the Modern Student*, 3d ed. (New York and Oxford: Oxford University Press, 1990), 438.

13 Smith, Address at Mobile, March 30, 1861, 10–11.

14 Oldham, Speech on Resolutions, January 20, 1865, 3.

15 Chambers, Speech on his resolution, November 10, 1864, 4.

CHAPTER THREE

Uncertainty in Definition:
The Rhetoric of 1861

IN THE spring and summer of 1861, before the Civil War unleashed its extreme violence and bloodshed, before economic deprivation and territorial loss sapped morale, the citizens of the Confederate States of America exulted over their new country and boasted of its abilities. They rejoiced that military victories in Virginia and Missouri substantiated claims of Confederate inviolability and speculated about how quickly and painlessly the South might attain complete independence. Furthermore, as events unfolded in favor of the Confederacy, the fear-mongers and the reluctant secessionists came to terms with and began to support the dissolution of the old United States. Men like Sam Houston of Texas, whose strong opposition to secession had once earned him the enmity of many in his state, by spring was speaking favorably for the South and its actions. On May 10, before an audience in his home state, Houston acknowledged that "The time has come when a man's section is his country." He also called for the South, "chivalric, brave, and impetuous as it is," to maintain its position until its independence was recognized.[1]

Euphoria translated into expressions of confidence and defiance in several modes of communication. Diarists boasted of the southern fighting ability while other, more gregarious writers filled newspapers with fiery editorials. William Nugent, a Mississippi planter, expressed his feelings in a letter. "I feel that I would like to shoot a Yankee," he wrote to his wife, ". . . The North will yet suffer for this fratricidal war she has forced upon us—Her fields will be desolated, her cities laid waste, and the treasures of her citizens dissipated in the vain attempt to subjugate a free people."[2] Dramatic and emotional words also came from hundreds of itinerant southern orators who amplified popular enthusiasm through energetic speeches. "Talk about *subjugating* us!" screamed a Georgia speaker to great applause, "Why, we might lay aside the men, and all Abolitiondom *couldn't run down the women even!*"[3] Together, the writers and speakers of 1861 produced a clear message; the South, united, able, and strong, would not be defeated.

Defiance, though, came packaged in bold statements that were at once exhilarating and misleading. When Robert Smith told a crowd at Mobile in April that "We are now a nation" and predicted the future held the "development of commerce, of manufactures, of arts," he misconstrued the actual conditions facing the country.[4] The South had not yet faced a major test of its strength, ability, or its conviction to the cause. That would come in fall and winter, 1861, as it faced growing economic problems and supply shortages, and in 1862, with the first major territorial losses. Like those who made unthinking boasts that the South could "*never be conquered,*" Smith expressed presumptions that some Confederates were willing to believe, but that were completely without foundation.[5]

The words were effective, however. They drew cheers in 1861 and today seem to accord with conventional wisdom about the Confederate mindset at the start of the war. A number of historians have depicted this period as a time of innocence, when a spirit of unity and a naive optimism emerged from several winter months of regional disagreement, uncertainty, and suspicion. Paul Escott incorporated this interpretation into *After Secession: Jefferson Davis and the Failure of Confederate Nationalism.* Writing about May, 1861, he said that "A wave of excitement and enthusiasm replaced the hesitation which had gone before as men welcomed the prospect of action. During the secession crisis, many southern leaders had boasted that any war with the North would be brief and victorious. Encouraged by these predictions, southerners now organized for war. In every state preparations went forward, and eager young men banded into companies." By the end of July, he adds, "The Confederate capital took on a carnival atmosphere, and the entire Confederacy experienced a great increase in confidence and élan." Studying the feelings of young men on both sides, James Robertson, Jr., in *Soldiers Blue and Gray*, wrote that "Northerners and Southerners went off to war with dreamy enthusiasm and youthful innocence. A nationwide belief existed in the spring of 1861 that one or two battles . . . would settle the whole issue." And the writers of *Why the South Lost the Civil War* have stated that a "mass psychology" in 1861 initially enabled southerners to stand "at the brink of the unknown and jump . . . resolutely and unsoberly." Through these works and many others, the year 1861 has often been organized into a pattern in which initial disharmony gives way to enthusiasm, which eventually yields before grim reality.[6]

Rhetorical analysis, however, reveals a far more complex scenario. Though southerners did write and speak generously of themselves in 1861, pontification amounted to only part of their message. Their second purpose, quieter than the exaggerated optimism expressed in the spring and summer, involved instruction and attention to uncertainty. Properly analyzed, the same words that proclaimed victory, shouted praise, and broadcast defiance also described a nation fraught with doubt and confusion. They tell that southerners did not suddenly and confidently transform themselves into Confederates, but assumed the new identity slowly, and with many questions.

Attention to uncertainty is especially evident in the oratory from mid-1861, for much of what orators said in the spring and summer sought to clarify issues and settle confusion. This side of Confederate oratory is easily lost amid emotion and hyperbole, but analysis locates it in phrasing and technique. Rhetorical examination reveals that many of the speeches delivered in the Confederacy's first months were saturated with definition, a technique of argument designed specifically to clarify information.

Quite common in Confederate oratory, definition has received a fair amount of treatment from rhetorical scholars. It often appears as a straightforward classification like Robert Smith's "We are now a nation," or like Sam Houston's flat statement that "a vindictive war is about to be inaugurated."[7] When definition appears, however, it generally carries certain implications. Several rhetoricians have noted that its presence suggests the existence of discord within an audience. According to Kenneth Burke, the act of "identification" or of defining similarities between individuals, generally implies the existence of division. "Identification," he said, "is affirmed with earnestness precisely because there is division. Identification is compensatory to division. If men were not apart from one another, there would be no need for the rhetorician to proclaim their unity."[8] Kathryn M. Olson added in a 1989 article that speakers use definition not only "to promote identification," but also to "advocat[e] adherence to the particular definition and

the perspective sponsoring it."[9] And Edward J. Corbett described
the use of definition as "a way of unfolding what is wrapped up in
a subject being examined. One of the rhetorical uses of [definition]
is to ascertain the specific issue to be discussed" in order that the
audience will clearly understand the arguments of the orator.[10]
Instances of definition, therefore, may serve as markers for subjects greeted with division or uncertainty.

That Confederate speeches from 1861 were especially packed
with definition suggests that many things were unclear during the
new nation's first year. Indeed, speakers' use of the technique was
so pervasive that even the simplest speeches—a few words in
response to a serenade, the brief pep talk of the third speaker at a
rally—generally included several attempts to explain one or more
issues. The degree to which definition could encompass and com-
plicate the message of an oration is illustrated in a speech from
Richmond, Virginia. In the early Summer, 1861, a unit of Maryland
volunteers arrived in Richmond to receive a battle flag. On June 8,
during the flag ceremony for "Soldiers of the Maryland Line," Mr.
James Mason spoke to the assembled troops. Because Mason was
to honor the men with a "soldier's welcome," he addressed them
with praise and enthusiasm.

"By your enterprise, your bravery, and your determined will,"
he began, "you have escaped from the thralldom of tyranny. . ."
Throughout the oration, he lauded their courage and the unselfish
devotion that brought them out of Maryland and into Virginia. He
asserted that their sacrifice would be known to history, and their
legacy one of honor. "When history records the transactions of this
epoch," Mason said with confidence, "when the passions of men
shall have subsided, and the historian can take a calm and philo-
sophical view of the events which have led to the present collision
. . . he will write that the people of the Southern States understood
and protected civil liberty." And soon, he added, the Marylanders

could expect to take their flag "back to Baltimore, unfurl it in your streets, and challenge the applause of your citizens."[11]

Mason's optimistic words enlivened his audience and provoked cheers and outbursts of clapping. The soldiers enthusiastically accepted his praise and predictions of victory; they shouted back to him in agreement. And between ovations, they also absorbed his instruction, for as he praised, Mason explained to a group of men away from home what was happening to them and to their world. He delivered, in other words, the aspect of 1861 oratory that has been neglected, the inconspicuous side that taught and soothed, all the while overshadowed by hyperbole and excitement. Properly analyzed, the tenor of Mason's words change. Many of his cheerful statements were, in fact, definitions, attempts to clarify recent events and address the uncertainty brought about by change.

During the speech, Mason attended to any doubts the soldiers might have had about Virginia. Speaking on behalf of the citizens of Richmond, Mason defined the attitudes the Marylanders could expect to encounter in the city: "We all know who you are. We all know what brought you here, and we are all ready, as I trust you have experienced, to extend to you a soldier's welcome." Paragraphs later, he expanded this definition to depict the city itself as the perfect station for incoming soldiers. "You are in Richmond," he said. "What is Richmond? It is a large city—a city of gallant men and refined women; . . . At the present moment, however, Richmond is a huge camp, where but one mind, one heart, and one determination animates every occupant, man, woman, and child."[12] These words taught that though the soldiers were in a new place, the people around them were united in their support and approval. The Marylanders apparently agreed, for at this point, they momentarily stopped the speech with applause.

Mason also addressed the soldiers themselves. "Now, my countrymen," he asked, "why are you here? What has brought you across the border? What is your mission to Virginia?" His defining answers were equally straightforward: "You have arms in your hands; . . . You are here not merely to fight our battles. No, I am not so selfish as to presume that; but to fight the battles of civil liberty in behalf of the entire South. You are on a high mission." He explained their new identities as soldiers, making sure he did not inflate the level of change in their lives: "[Y]ou are volunteers for the war, and you are volunteers for the great cause of the South against the aggressions of the North. You are no strangers; you are our neighbors."

Mason also defined what lay ahead, pointing out "You will have no child's play" and urging the men to "endure the trials of the camp; the weariness of the forced march; the vigilance of day and night; the restraints of discipline, and the patience to bear with discomforts and disappointments. This," he stated, "is the real test of courage . . ."[13] Mason's speech thus illustrates the dual nature of 1861 oratory. Its stirring words promoted enthusiasm and confidence, but its definitions addressed uncertainty and doubt. People with questions about the presence of Maryland soldiers, and soldiers themselves unclear about their surroundings and actions, could find answers and resolution within the discourse.

Mason's approach was hardly unique. Indeed, many other speeches and sermons were similarly structured, indicating that the defiant and boastful words that rang from podiums, pulpits, and lecterns across the South had a similar disposition. All were cheerful facades that disguised the serious work of explanation and instruction.[14]

To expose completely the level of uncertainty in Confederate society during the so-called optimistic months of spring and summer, one need only study the amazing array of definitions contained in the oratory. So much, in fact, seemed in need of elucidation that speakers ended up defining a complete portrait of their country, a portrait that included everything from abstract political philosophies to the role of the lady in war.

These definitions reflected how speakers conceived of the Confederacy and what they felt their audiences would accept. For example, regarding the South's role in the breakup of the Union, a number of orators cast their region as blameless. Many sounded like Alabama minister H. N. Pierce. In a June sermon titled "God Our Only Trust," he defined how disunion actually reflected southern responsibility. "We claim our rights—nothing more," he said. "We have separated ourselves for peace-sake. Thirty years of misunderstandings, heart-burnings and bickerings, have shown that it is far better for all concerned, that we should be no longer one people. We have quietly withdrawn, and relieved them from all responsibility with regard to Southern institutions. . . . We desire peace. We ask only to be left in quiet. If war comes, it is of their own seeking . . ."[15]

And war seemed inevitable, for, as many speakers pointed out, the South, gentle and peaceful as it was, did not exist in a world of its own choosing. It had an enemy, a "dastardly foe" made up of "barbarian[s]," and "treacherous invader[s]" plotting to extend a "reign of oppression."[16] The enemy was the North, a region of fellow Americans less than a year earlier, now redefined as an oppressive antagonist, predatory, hunkered in ice and snow, and arrayed insidiously against the South. The North must have been a subject of particular concern, for many southern speeches on many different occasions involved its discussion. Henry Wise, in simply trying to say a few words to some serenaders, could not resist providing a lengthy definition of northern aggression: "They have undertaken to annul laws within your own limits. . . . They have abolitionized your border, as the disgraced Northwest will show. They have invaded your moral strongholds and the rights of your religion. . . . They have invaded the sanctity of your homes and firesides, and endeavored to play master, father, and husband for you in your households. . . . [T]he armies of the invader are hovering around the tomb of Washington."[17] These and other, similar words resolved uncertainty over the new relationship between North and South. No longer two parts of one country, in the orators' portrait the South became a peaceful, quiet land and the North a vicious and unrelenting predator.

Concerns over how to defeat such an enemy were addressed in detail. Orators defined a variety of strengths and a complete range of behaviors and attitudes that, if properly implemented, ensured success. They spoke bluntly about conduct, often sounding like Howell Cobb when he flatly told a Georgia audience "I'll tell you what you can do and what you are expected to do."[18] Across the South, audiences learned that independence from the North came with terrific demands on their conduct. Speakers defined temperance, obedience to authority, virtue, frugality, bravery, pride, discipline, sacrifice, and fortitude as some of the many traits evident in the model Confederate citizen. Strength of character made the South unconquerable, for, as one speaker explained, "Nothing but convictions of truth and devotion to right ever yet gave, in the long run, victory to a nation or an individual. Leaving out of the question the mere power by which it is supported, falsehood contains the elements of its own dissolution."[19] Northerners might have economic strength and great manpower, but southerners would always prevail, their superior nature providing an eternal advantage.

Speakers also bolstered southern morale by defining the Confederate cause as superior, even ethereal. Southerners fought a "war of purification" and passed through a "fiery baptism."[20] "They are," stated one Virginian in April, "contending for everything dear to the hearts of freemen and fair women; . . . for liberty, for right, for manhood, for truth; they are contending for the her-

45

itage of freedom transmitted to them by their revolutionary forefathers, and it is impossible that their cause should miscarry."[21] The righteousness of the southern cause attracted two powerful allies that sanctioned the South's actions and prevented misfortune. Describing southerners as protagonists in a battle between liberty and tyranny, speakers linked their actions to those of guardians of freedom dating back to ancient times. "I have chosen a text once prayed by a man who often was in a similar situation as ours," said a minister in South Carolina, in reference to David, the Biblical hero.[22] Others described how Christians defied Roman emperors and suffered for their faith, noting that the religion nonetheless survived and eventually prospered. And many spoke of the Revolutionary War, when a few American patriots stood against the might of the British empire and achieved independence for thirteen North American colonies. For centuries men had fought for and achieved what was just and right, sometimes against tremendous odds. Speakers defined these individuals as heroes, cast southerners as the heirs to their tradition of courage, and garnered the support of history for the South.[23]

Paired with the might of history, divine sanction also benefited the South. The Confederacy received the protection and support of God, and in turn, tried to carry out His measures. "And such is the condition of this country!" explained Louisiana's Reverend John Gierlow in an August sermon, ". . . True, the Lord is 'our help and our shield.' We have put our trust in His holy name, and He has fought our battles. . . . O, let us stand in awe before His throne of Mercy!"[24] Evidence of divine blessing was said to come from the many favors God bestowed on the South, such as its natural abundance and the slave labor force, described as a "blessing to mankind."[25]

The ringing words voiced in 1861 indicate that the spring and

summer after secession a more complex time than has been recognized, for even as Confederate orators spoke boldly of the South
and secession, they also addressed uncertainty over their nation's
past and future, and helped citizens establish new identities as
Confederates. Speakers sought to define a new nation, a
Confederacy that arose from the responsible efforts of a victimized
people. They talked of how it existed peacefully and quietly,
blessed by God, full of rich land and happy labor, and populated
by a brave, giving, and united people. Danger loomed from the
North, where a savage and powerful enemy lurked, but southerners were confident of their ability to prevail, bolstered by their
place in history and sanctioned by God. The portrait also included
definitions of the Confederate government, Confederate women,
weapons, fighting techniques, farming methods, and the nation's
economic status, all subjects speakers apparently believed were
clouded in confusion and uncertainty.

Rhetorical analysis thus questions some long-standing historical interpretations about the first months of Confederacy. High
levels of definition in the oratory from 1861 suggest the presence of
a fair amount of confusion and doubt. Had Confederates felt
supremely confident and completely resolute in their actions, they
would have had no need for speakers' repeated definitions. But the
need was there, and Confederates by the thousands flocked to
hear the words and explanations of their orators.

The next step in studying Confederate oratory, however, involves
expanding the analysis to involve all the rhetorical techniques
available, including figures of speech, and the full array of arguments. An examination of Confederate rhetoric in general through
1865 will determine the themes that emerged during four years of
Civil War, discover how these themes were initially defined, and
study how well early definitions withstood the test of war.

Notes

1 Sam Houston, Speech at Independence, Texas, May 10, 1861, in *Echoes from the South Comprising the Most Important Speeches, Proclamations, and Public Acts Emanating from the South during the Late War* (New York: E. B. Treat & Co., 1866), 175, 180.

2 John K. Bettersworth, ed., *Mississippi in the Confederacy as They Saw It*, Published for the Mississippi Department of Archives and History, Jackson, Mississippi (Baton Rouge: Louisiana State University Press, 1961), 63, quoting William L. Nugent to his wife, August 19, 1861.

3 Howell Cobb, Speech at Atlanta, Georgia, May 22, 1861, in *Echoes from the South*, 186.

4 Hon. Robert H. Smith, *An Address to the Citizens of Alabama on the Constitution and Laws of the Confederate States of America by the Honorable Robert H. Smith at Temperance Hall, on the 30th of March, 1861* (Mobile: Mobile Daily Register Print, 1861), 23.

5 Cobb, Speech at Atlanta, May 22, 1861, in *Echoes from the South*, 187

6 Paul D. Escott, *After Secession: Jefferson Davis and the Failure of Confederate Nationalism* (Baton Rouge and London: Louisiana State University Press, 1978), 44, 52; James I. Robertson, Jr., *Soldiers Blue and Gray*, American Military History Series, Thomas L. Connelly, ed. (Columbia: University of South Carolina Press, Warner Books Edition, 1988), 4; Richard E. Beringer, Herman Hathaway, Archer Jones, and William N. Still, Jr., *Why the South Lost the Civil War* (Athens and London: University of Georgia Press, 1986), 82. Actual quote is past tense. Also refer to works by W. Buck Yearns and Richard B. Harwell. Yearns, in *The Confederate Congress* (Athens: University of Georgia Press, 1960), 8, builds the picture of early enthusiasm inside the Confederate government: "James T. Harrison of Mississippi also reported that they were 'all in good spirits & firm in the faith;'" Howell Cobb spoke of "general good feeling and disposition to unite and harmonize on whatever may be found the best policy." Both quotes were from February, 1861. Richard B. Harwell, in *The Confederate Reader: How the South Saw the War* (New York: Dover Publications, Inc., 1989), 9, wrote as part of his introduction to "1861" that in the lower South, "enthusiasm and emotion overrode wise admonition. The wisdom and love for the old Union . . . could not prevail against the ambition-fired confidence and irresponsible claims of the fire-eaters."

7   Smith, Speech at Mobile, March 30, 1861, 23; Houston, Speech at Independence, May 10, 1861, in *Echoes from the South*, 178.

8   Kenneth Burke, *On Symbols and Society*, ed. Joseph R. Gusfield (Chicago and London: The University of Chicago Press, 1989), 181–82.

9   Kathryn M. Olson, "The Controversy over President Reagan's Visit to Bitburg: Strategies Of Definition and Redefinition," in *Quarterly Journal of Speech* 75 (1989): 131.

10 Edward P. J. Corbett, *Classical Rhetoric for the Modern Student*, 3d ed. (New York: Oxford University Press, 1990), 97.

11 J[ames] M[urray] Mason, Speech at Richmond, June 8, 1861, in *Echoes from the South*, 166, 167, 173.

12 *Ibid.*, 166, 170.

13 *Ibid.*, 168, 169, 171, 172.

14 For other examples of 1861 speeches that have high levels of definition, see William C. Butler, *Sermon Preached in St. John's Church, Richmond, Virginia, on the Sunday After the Battle at Mannassas, July 21, 1861, by the Rector* (Richmond: Chas. H. Wynne, Printer, 1861), in which Butler unleashed a string of definitions in regard to the Battle of First Manassas and God's role in military actions. Also, on June 13, 1861, the Reverend Ferdinand Jacobs defined a wide array of subjects ranging from the southern attitude towards God, to the future, to the southern war mentality, to the northern mindset, to the character necessary for victory, and more. He stated that "We, as a people, by our delegates in Convention assembled, . . . have made a devout recognition of Him as the Almighty God; we humbly express our dependence on him." Jacobs also pointed out that "our independence is not yet achieved. Our existence as a Nation is not yet established. We have yet, in all probability, to make our way through a destructive conflict." He claimed, "We would seek the gratification of no revenge," but noted that "fanaticism has possession of the great body of the people of the North . . ." Towards his conclusion, he defined the elements of character southerners needed to win the coming war. "In order to our enjoyment, of God's favor and protection, we must be a righteous people," he said. "His law must be honored; his authority must be recognized . ." Rev. Ferdinand Jacobs, *A Sermon, for the Times: Preached in Fairview Presbyterian Church, Perry County, Alabama, on Thursday, June 13, 1861– The Day of Fasting and Prayer, appointed by the Confederate Authorities, in View of the National Exigencies* (Published by request of the Congregation, Marion, AL, 1861), 5, 7.

15   H. N. Pierce, *Sermons Preached in St. John's Church, on the 13ᵗʰ of June, 1861, the National Fast, Appointed by his Excellency Jefferson Davis, President of the Confederate States of America* (Mobile: Farrow & Bennett, Book and Job Printers, 1861), 6. For an example of the South cast as a victim see Rev. L. Muller, Sermon at Institute Hall, on Fast Day, June 13, 1861, Delivered Before the German Military Companies and German Population, in *Charleston Daily Courier*, June 17, 1861. Muller said that the North was advocating "dictatorship," adopting a "threatening position . . . towards the South," desiring to "coerce and subjugate." Muller asked, "But could we quietly *stand* there, and not *defend* . . . with all our might?" See also Alexander Stephens, Speech at Augusta, Georgia, July 11, 1861, in *The Rebellion Record: A Diary of American Events with Documents, Narratives, Illustrative Incidents, Poetry, Etc.*, vol. 2 (New York: D. Van Nostrand, 1866), 276. Stephens said "unless we intend to be overridden and beaten down and subjugated, and to become the vassals of his mercenaries . . . we must every one of us . . . be prepared to do our duty."

16   Sergeant Welch, Speech in response to General Simons at the Anniversary of the Battle of Fort Moultrie, Charleston, South Carolina, delivered June 28, 1861, in *Charleston Daily Courier*, June 29, 1861.

17   Henry Wise, Speech in spring, 1861, at public meeting, location obscured, dated obscured, [Richmond, June 1, 1861], in *Milledgeville Federal Union*, June 11, 1861.

18   Howell Cobb, Speech at Atlanta, May 29(?), 1861, in *Milledgeville Federal Union*, June 4, 1861. For a similar statement ("Permit me . . . to depict the character of a model soldier"), see E. T. Winkler, *Duties of the Citizen Soldier. A Sermon Delivered in the First Baptist Church of Charleston, S.C., on Sabbath Morning, January 6, 1861, before the Moultrie Guards by E. T. Winkler, D. D., Chaplain of the Company* (Charleston: A. J. Burke, 1861), 10.

19   Reverend A. M. Randolph, *Address on the Day of Fasting and Prayer Appointed by the President of the Confederate States, June 13, 1861, Delivered in St. George's Church, Fredericksburg, Virginia* (Fredericksburg: The Recorder Job Office, 1861), 9.

20   Wise, Speech in spring, in *Milledgeville Federal Union*, June 11, 1861.

21   Roger Pryor, Speech at Charleston, April 10, 1861, in *Charleston Daily Courier*, April 11, 1861

22 Reverend L. Muller, Sermon at Institute Hall, on Fast Day, June 13, 1861, delivered before the German Military Companies and German Population, Charleston, South Carolina, in *Charleston Daily Courier*, June 17, 1861.

23 For other examples of historical figures cited as role models again see Reverend L. Muller, Sermon at Institute Hall, June 13, 1861. Muller also cited Gustavus Adolphus who came "to the assistance of the oppressed Protestants of Germany, and land[ed] with only 15,000 Swedes in Pomerania . . ." J[ames] Mason, on June 8, 1861, glorified the Maryland soldiers of the Revolution, stating, "We had, in the days of the first Revolution, a Maryland line, whose name has passed into history without one blot upon its fair escutcheon—a Maryland line who illustrated upon every field in the South their devotion to the civil liberty of that day. . . . They were your ancestry. They traveled barefooted, unclothed, without blankets or tents, and but few muskets, and you came after them." (169)

24 J. Gierlow, Sermon. A View of the Present Crisis. By Reverend J. Gierlow, Rector of St. James Church, Baton Rouge (n. p., n. d.) source unknown, 7.

25 Reverend W. H. Watkins, The South, Her Position and Duty. A Discourse Delivered at the Methodist Church, Natchez, Mississippi, January 4, 1861 (N. d., n. p.), in Mississippi Department of Archives and History, Jackson, Mississippi, 5.

CHAPTER FOUR

From Sacred to Sinister Depictions of Nature

BY THE summer of 1861, with secession complete and open warfare with the North underway, Confederate orators began the process of developing a detailed image of their nation, a task which
noticeably altered the character of their discourse. In the atmosphere of excitement and uncertainty during March through June,
many speeches had been bluntly prescriptive, relying on the exor-
bitant and forthright use of definition to provide an immediate, if
inelegant, explanation of the Confederacy and its people. But as
southerners proved themselves in battle, grew accustomed to their
new status, and realized an abundant fall harvest, the intense feelings of the spring abated and familiar emotions returned to the
region. Soldiers wrote of how their initial excitement for military
service faded, and boredom took its place.[1] One South Carolinian
noted in August that "the orators, the spouters, the furious patriots
that could hardly be held, who were so unduly anxious to do or die

for their country" seemingly vanished after the battle at First Manassas.[2] And, in oratory, greater variety in argument and style joined the mostly instructive rhetoric of early 1861.

The expanded style of discourse involved, among other things, an increase in the use of metaphor, a figure of speech through which items of different nature and significance are joined in order to create an image for the audience. Metaphor was one of the most common devices in Confederate oratory, one that appeared in all types of discourse and in regard to a wide array of subjects. Therefore, in order to apprehend fully the words of southern orators, one must understand how metaphor functions in discourse. Towards this end, a 1983 article by rhetorician Michael Leff has been of particular value.

Studying how metaphor works upon human thought, Leff pointed out that scholars have traditionally classified it as a mere ornament, a device suitable for briefly sparking the imagination, but not as weighty or complex as the forms of argument. In argument, it was believed, a speaker drew his audience through various steps of logic and reasoning, raising their thought, and helping them to order and understand his beliefs and conclusions. With metaphor, he merely set up a striking juxtaposition that briefly fixed attention on an unusual comparison, thus decorating his prose with an imaginative aside. In Leff's words, the traditional interpretation erected a "wall of separation" between metaphor and argument.[3]

With the development of interaction theory in the 1960s, however, rhetoricians, though not detracting from metaphor's stylistic aspects, began to suggest that the device did not simply decorate, but instead functioned in a complex manner similar to that of argument.[4] Summarizing the ideas of several scholars, Leff wrote that speech analysts have recently come to believe that audiences comprehend a metaphoric statement as the two juxtaposed items "interact with one another, and various aspects of these subjects are selected, emphasized, suppressed, and ordered."[5] In other words, interaction theorists postulate that when people hear a metaphorical statement, instead of receiving it superficially as a type of ornament, they comprehend the imagery only after studying and ordering the associated objects much in the same way that they analyze the points of an argument.

Interaction theory is significant to this essay because it illustrates the link between metaphor and society. The idea that audiences select, emphasize, and order "various aspects" of the items juxtaposed suggests that they bring a collection of personal ideas and images into their interpretation. According to rhetoricians, audiences surround each item in the metaphor with a number of "associated commonplaces," images and beliefs that automatically come to mind when the item is presented. In order for a metaphor to be effective, therefore, the speaker must juxtapose items that fall within the common experience of his audience or risk their misinterpreting his meaning. Leff made this point succinctly. "Metaphor," he stated, "draws its materials from communal knowledge."[6]

When this interpretation is applied to Confederate oratory, it indicates that southerners readily understood imagery about two subjects in particular: slavery and nature. Slavery will be the topic of a later chapter. This chapter concerns the rhetorical treatment of the southern landscape and of the region's natural phenomena, for references to these subjects, framed metaphorically or otherwise, occurred frequently in Confederate oratory.

In fact, a survey of southern Civil War discourse reveals that speakers mentioned the natural environment in virtually every type of oration. In speeches before soldiers, they compared men to "trees transplanted into another soil," and warned of the approaching "storm of battle."[7] Standing in the halls of state legislatures and in the national Congress, political orators spoke of green fields, the sea, howling storms, and mountains, often pairing natural imagery with serious argument. And in church, ministers spoke readily about soil, water, mountains, storms, and fire. The Reverend John Parks, for example, attempted to raise spirits in 1864 by pointing out that though the wicked might "flourish as a green bay tree for awhile, yet the eye of God is upon him and retribution must and will overtake him."[8] References to the natural environment even appeared in some of the desperate orations delivered late in the war. At a mass meeting in March, 1865, Governor Watts of Alabama cried that the Confederacy rejected "ignominious terms of peace presented to us by Lincoln" with "the sound of mighty waters."[9]

Such consistent inclusion of the natural environment produced a type of rhetoric in which detailed references to the southern landscape, climate, and even rare phenomena were common. In their use of metaphor, for example, speakers expected listeners to properly interpret juxtapositions involving specific types of trees, as well as, among other things, pebbles, whirlpools, thunderstorms, galaxies, clouds, the ocean, mountains, bears, locusts, birds, and leaves. They also referred directly to distant rivers, mountains, unusual vegetables, climatic conditions, and soil. In rhetoric, the frequency with which orators mention a subject registers their confidence about its suitability. Judging from the pandemic occurrence of the environment in Confederate rhetoric, southern speakers apparently felt that their countrymen understood the South's landscape and weather conditions in detail.

And, given the mentality of many southerners before the war, this assumption was not implausible. A number of historians have pointed out that antebellum southerners, because they lived primarily in rural settings, became acutely sensitive to their surroundings. Bertram Wyatt-Brown portrayed planters and farmers as inevitably linked to the natural cycles of "death and birth–the violence of hog-killing, the tasks of calving . . ." Southerners, he said, interpreted these events as "all part of the same comforting routines and duties. They were life itself."[10] And William Freehling described how residents of the Deep South so internalized their surroundings that their conversations inevitably turned to "hurricanes and floods, the price of cotton and of slaves, cost of land and yield per acre, making a killing before cotton killed the soil."[11]

Southerners, in fact, not only talked incessantly about their natural environment, but they also discussed the subject in their letters, diaries, and newspapers. Traveling in the North, as was fashionable before the war, they studied and wrote about the landscape, feeling, according to historian John Hope Franklin, "well qualified to comment on the physical features of the northern countryside. Even if they lived in a southern town or city, they had some familiarity with the southern countryside, through their own plantations or other rural connections, that had sharpened their powers to observe any rural scene . . ."[12] In addition, planters kept journals about crops, soil conditions, and climatic developments, noting periods of drought and rain and recording their thoughts about the appearance of their crops and their countryside.

In many cases, these journals provide in-depth information about the physical characteristics of the American South, for some writers, like farmer David Golightly Harris, were prolific note-takers. Harris, from the South Carolina piedmont, has been described as an "average slaveholder," a man who by 1860 farmed 100 acres and owned ten bondsmen, most of whom worked outdoors in field and lumber work.[13] Despite the relatively small size of his operation, however, Harris took great interest in his lands and crops. He wrote daily about the weather, taking note of clouds, rain, and cold spells, even differentiating between "light frost" and "really white . . . frost & ice." He studied his corn, wheat, and oat crops, recorded the growth in his gardens ("Had wattermelons [sic], roasting corn, and a few nutmeg melons"), discussed hunting for turkeys, foxes, beehives, and wild fruits, and generally agonized over his soils and the condition of his lands. His journal entries typically included information about both weather and crops. For April 28, 1858, for example, he noted, "Last [night] was quite cold. . . . All of our beans have been killed and some potatoe, cabbage. . . . Two hands replanting corn at the Mountain. This corn is much frost-bitten, but I think it will come out again. The day is quite cold."[14]

Southern novels and newspapers further illustrate regional interest in the natural environment, for these mediums also described the countryside and took note of a variety of natural occurrences. Opening the *Memphis Daily Appeal* on January 10, 1857, readers found not only a report of "snow!" in Mississippi, but also a short, metaphorical filler juxtaposing human life with the climatic condition known as "Indian summer." "In the life of a good man," it read, "there is an Indian summer more beautiful than that of the seasons; richer, sunnier, more sublime than the most glorious Indian summer."[15] Chapter One of the popular antebellum novel *Swallow Barn* offered a lengthy description of a Virginia landscape, of an "extensive tract of land which stretches some three or four miles along the river, presenting alternately abrupt promontories mantled with pine and dwarf oak, and small inlets terminating in swamps."[16] According to literary scholar Jan Bakker, the antebellum southern romances of several male authors included "pastoral imagery" of "pleasant groves, flower-perfumed air," and graceful fields."[17]

But the southern environment was far more paradoxical than its advocates suggested, for amid beauty and splendor lurked impassable swamps, mud, thick undergrowth, dangerous insects, and deadly reptiles.[18] Some sections looked ugly and presented enormous difficulties for farming; logging often transformed expansive forests into barren, eroded fields, while inattention to drainage allowed floods and rains to reduce lands to muddy wastes. Environmental historian Albert E. Cowdry also adds that expanses of southern soils were mediocre for farming, and that "melodramatic" weather, including tornadoes, hurricanes, and hailstorms, ravaged the landscape.[19]

Southerners acknowledged the limitations and destructive forces of their natural environment in several ways. Newspapers found dramatic value in lightning strikes and terrible storms, and farmers spent a fair amount of time complaining. Harris griped about high heat and droughts, about "These awful, dark thunderstorms . . . so common that I am getting tired of them," and about rains and frost that spoiled his crops.[20] And some also took steps to remedy the shortcomings of their region. Planters attended agricultural lectures and read journal articles describing ways in which increased output might be wrung from what a Carolinian called "the little remnant of fertility still left in our lands."[21] States assisted by passing laws restricting burning and logging activity.

Like antebellum southerners, Confederate orators acknowledged the contradictions in their surroundings. As Silas Bunch pointed out, "these skies, now so balmy and benignant, shall, 'ere we are scarce aware, be terrible with the rush of the hurricane, and the dismal blaze of the forked lightening [sic], and the awful roar of the thunder . . ."[22] However, in 1861 and 1862, many speakers declined to place environmental limitations or dangers within the Confederacy. Instead, they attached these features to other areas of the world, often with the implication that natural disturbances and instability visited regions tainted by social improprieties.

The North, therefore, was frequently defined as a land of "bleak snows," and "frozen seas," as a frightening region threatened by snakes, deadly lightning, "gibbering spirits," walls of fire, whirlwinds, and the "storm clouds of Abolition fanaticism."[23] Mexico was an inhospitable desert of "burning sands."[24] Europe, according to one South Carolina speaker, rocked under the "throes of earthquakes," shook before the "sweep of ten thousand storms," and lay in waste from the "gloomy track of the tornado."[25] Italy contained a dangerous volcano; Africa subjected its people to "enervating heats and destructive fevers," and India was described as "ravaged as with a storm of fire!"[26] Sometimes references to nature even indicate the presence of interstate rivalries within the Confederacy. In one instance, a Texas speaker identified natural flaws in regions that bordered his state. New Mexico, according to Judge Thomas J. Devine, featured "arid plains" and "bleak hills." He also stated that as Texas soldiers marched to Virginia, they first had to pass through the "low prairies and 'trembling lands' of Louisiana, wading and marching through mud and water . . . in dripping garments, suffering far greater privations than the soldiers of the Revolution on their march to Valley Forge."[27]

In contrast, though, most orators spoke of the South's gentle climate and terrain of unmatched beauty and majesty, and only occasionally referred to its tired soil and unpredictable weather. Speaking of their own environment, orators defined its size and variety of vegetation, but often exchanged instructive language for a more jubilant style of communication.[28] "What a noble, inviting country!" cried a speaker in April, 1861. "What a soil, and climate, and variety of productions. . . . almost everywhere an inviting soil, capable of every variety of production, and, in many portions of the Confederacy, still of virgin fertility—with every good climate in the world, and very little of the bad . . ."[29] In Georgia, Howell Cobb avoided telling his listeners what to think about their environment and only urged them to recognize its plenty. "Heaven has smiled upon us from the first," he shouted from a hotel balcony. "Go and look at your crops; you may call it a good season, or whatever else you may, but I tell you that it is the blessing of God upon us at this time."[30] Cobb's link between the environment and the divine was not unusual; many speakers claimed that natural grandeur reflected the blessings of God.[31]

Having dispatched frightening natural occurrences beyond the borders of their country, orators focused more on the Confederacy's bounty and beautiful features, often linking natural abundance to national power and strength. "The wealth of our country is immense and its prospective resources are inexhaustible fountains of public credit," stated a Virginian in March, 1862, ". . . we shall see that our power is unbroken and substantially unimpaired. . . . Our country presents many natural advantages for defense, . . . Climate also contests an invasion of our country. The roads themselves swallow up the power of an invader."[32]

In seeking to link the environment and the nation, most speakers tried to be as detailed in their descriptions as possible. None, however, approached the level of specification reached by Richard Yeadon in an August, 1862 speech in Aiken, South Carolina. Before the war, Aiken's fame rested primarily in its congenial climate and beautiful setting. Citizens from Charleston spent summers there, exchanging their city's heat and humidity for clean air and a gentle climate. Invalids visited as well, hoping to recover their health amid the town's hundreds of trees, flowers, and orchards. Plants of all types grew wonderfully in Aiken; fruit did especially well, and plums, apricots, nectarines, and strawberries were available in abundance. In 1858, recognizing their good fortune, town citizens formed an agricultural society to "promote the culture and improve the quality of fruit in general."[33] It was this society that asked Mr. Yeadon, editor of the *Charleston Courier*, to speak.

Addressing the South Carolina Vine Growing and Horticultural Association, Yeadon argued that gardening illustrated a high level of civilization. And, in order to prove that the South exemplified advanced cultural development, he launched into an exhaustive portrait of Confederate cultivation, a portrait that drew on the gardens, crops, and orchards of Aiken:

> [W]e have the apricot, the nectarine, the pear, the apple, the plum, the cherry, the fig and the quince. Here too, the strawberry, bordering beds with green and rich leaved fringe, . . . aided by the dairy, supplies the delicious bowl of strawberries and cream, . . . the raspberry . . . and the grape vine, twining the frequent arbor, or climbing the trellis, and clinging to them with its curling tendrils, like a woman's love to a man's support . . .
>
> Nor must I omit to mention the kitchen garden and its store of vegetable wealth. The exquisite marrow of the asparagus, the *hard*-headed cabbage, . . . the golden carrot; the richly colored and well flavored watermelon, and the luscious muskmelon and cantaloupe, the curious kohl-rabbi, with its turnip bulb above ground, . . . the delicate squash, common and cushaw, the Guinea squash or egg plant, the green corn in the ear, . . . okra and tomatoes . . . are among the vegetable treasures, which careful and assiduous culture wrests in great perfection from our sandy soil.[34]

Confederate speakers celebrated and aggrandized their environment through 1861 and well into 1862. Audiences, according to newspapers, responded enthusiastically with the "wildest applause" and vociferous cheers.[35] But, there was a danger in placing such emphasis on natural beauty and bounty during a time of war, a danger relating to the character of war and its effects on the natural world. Military conflict changes the environment in devastating and shocking ways; smoke from the guns and fires of battle obscures the sky; fields are laid waste, and trees scarred by bullets. Waters run with blood and choke with bodies, while gentle breezes turn acrid from the effects of gunpowder and explosives. During the early stages of conflict, in 1861 and 1862, by envisioning and celebrating their country solely in terms of its majesty and plenty, southerners failed to prepare themselves for the possibility of its destruction, or for an existence in surroundings made ugly by combat.

To be sure, a few speakers had warned that natural disturbances could appear in the South should the region depart from the correct path. John A. Gilmer, a North Carolina unionist who considered secession illegal, described the South in January 1861, as in the clutches of a "raging storm."[36] The Reverend H. N. Pierce cautioned Alabamians that if they were to lose their respect for God, "the rain of heaven should be withheld for a few months." Or, "Instead of a drought, if the showers of Heaven should descend much more copiously than usual, the worm might make its appearance in our fields . . ."[37] A few speakers also pointed out that war could affect their nation's beauty and alluded to the possibility of environmental destruction. However, a greater number focused enthusiastically on their country's natural majesty and strength, and this behavior indicates that audiences did not gladly receive warnings about the future.[38] Confederates apparently did not care to hear suggestions that they might suffer or fail in war. They preferred words like those delivered by a graduation speaker in Richmond, Virginia, statements that the South, with "a broad, and fertile land, with many a mountain pass for a Thermopylae and many a plain for a Marathon," could not be defeated. "The attempts to subjugate such a country," he said, "must be as futile as an attempt to subdue the waves of the ocean . . ."[39]

However, in 1862, southerners were forced to confront the destruction and loss of their territory. Large tracts of land burned in the battle of Shiloh (April), and areas of Tennessee, North Carolina, and Louisiana fell to the North. Sections of the Mississippi River, once called a "mighty stream" of "majesty," "grandeur," and "power," became a northern waterway and, in Baton Rouge, a garbage pit for the remains of cotton burned in advance of the approaching Union army (May).[40] For Virginians, the Peninsular Campaign (April–July) turned their "sacred soil" into fodder for pillaging northern forces, while fighting in Fredericksburg (December) turned the battlefield into a "horrible spectacle" of bodies and blood.[41] Soldiers tore into the land to make trenches, showered it with shells, fired crops, and trampled gardens. After the war, a northerner traveled to an 1864 battle site in Virginia and noted the devastation of the land, how "only a ghostly grove of dead [tree] trunks and dreary dry limbs remained." Riding near the site of the "Bloody Angle" at Spotsylvania Court House, he noticed a "hacked and barkless trunk . . . in the midst of graves."[42] In 1866, farmers plowed skulls from the ground at Antietam.

Discourse from late 1862 and to the end of the Civil War indicates that the war forced southerners to reconsider what they believed about their surroundings. Initially, speakers were unable to unite on a single solution or set of instructions as to how citizens should react to their changing world. Governor Zebulon Vance of North Carolina told the people of his state to "suffer and endure" and to rethink their concept of the environment as a land of plenty. "All the fruits of the earth," he said, "should be saved most carefully; retrenchment and reform should begin in our households . . ."[43] William Yancey suggested that Confederates transform their surroundings into a battlement, "to make of each hill-top a fort, of each pass an ambuscade, and of each plain a battle-field."[44] And Benjamin Hill offered no plan of action at all, preferring instead to maintain the image of a beautiful and strong environment, reassuring his listeners that "we [have] a territory not surpassed by any nation—large, compact, and fertile," and describing the land as the "flowing gardens of beautiful Pensacola;

... the wave-washed shore of surf-beaten Hatteras; ... the banks of the classic James and York."[45]

However, through 1863, with warfare growing more destructive and northern forces moving relentlessly into Confederate territory, orators devoted increasing attention to a new, darker concept of their environment. And, in a speech from September, 1862, Williamson Oldham expressed himself in a way that anticipated this change in attitude. Oldham urged southerners to make bloodshed and destruction their impetus to fight harder. Noting that Confederate soldiers had "met the enemy on a hundred bloody fields," he used a metaphor suggestive of natural destruction, the metaphor of fire, to press for increased fighting spirit and bloodlust. Urging his countrymen to "fan the flame to brighter burning," he subtly indicated that natural destruction did not matter, that flames, the natural enemy of forests and plains, should be increased and more "bloody fields" created.[46] With these words, Oldham presaged a coming shift in Confederate thought, for, faced with the destruction and loss of their land, southerners began to speak against their natural environment. In many cases, they ceased to describe natural beauty and began casting the environment as ugly and antagonistic.

This change in attitude is manifest in several aspects of rhetoric. In their use of metaphor, for example, speakers increasingly began joining unfriendly elements of nature with the Confederacy, a process that suggests audiences were becoming aware of the dangers in their surroundings and less interested in flowers, plants, and sunbeams. One man said that the nation was caught in the "whirlpool of Revolution" and balanced on the edge of an "unfathomed chasm," with a "yawning gulf!"[47] In 1863, a speaker in Congress referred to an "ocean of blood" that threatened to swallow the South's republican government, leaving dictatorship in its place.[48] One year later, Governor Vance of North

Carolina spoke metaphorically about a "roaring flood" that nearly drowned the citizens of his state, while a minister in Richmond, Virginia, talked of how "monsters as moral sharks, vultures, and vampires have flourished upon the ruin of the land."[49] Other speakers juxtaposed the Confederacy with hoar-frost, reptiles, dark clouds, and dangerous animals.

Besides metaphor, other elements of rhetoric also indicate that southerners became increasing gloomy about their natural environment as the war progressed. Rhetorical questions evocative of natural destruction and deterioration began to appear. While a speaker in 1861 cheerily asked "has not South Carolina holy ground for you?"[50] a military officer in late 1863 sought to convey a very different feeling. "How is it with us?" he asked. "Half our territory overrun. . . . smoking ruins, and plantations abandoned and laid waste, meet us on all sides, and anarchy and ruin, disappointment and discontent lower over all the land!"[51]

Speakers used comparisons to examine the devastation around them in detail. Mr. Perkins, of Louisiana, contrasted the state of the Mississippi River before and after the war, pointing out that the destruction of its "immense levees," once of such grandeur as to attract foreign tourists, now allowed the waterway to rampage through fields nearly fifty miles outside of its regular route.[52] And finally, the words associated with the environment began to change. In many speeches, the "sacred soil" and "holy ground" of 1861 and 1862 took on a new, grotesque status. Speakers during the latter years of the war referred variously to their land as desolate, crumbling, ruined, "laid waste," "sown with blood," covered with "bones . . . bleaching upon its plains."[53] In October 1863, General E. W. Gantt of Arkansas even cast the southern environment as the Confederate soldier's enemy. Its snow and ice froze his "half-clad" body, and he "shivered under the bleak sky." Furthermore, its "scene of blackness, of anguish, and desolation . . . where wealth, happiness, and plenty [once] smiled" destroyed confidence and bred depression.[54] As Albert G. Brown of Mississippi acknowledged in late 1863, the environment was becoming a source of despair. Studying the land, he sighed, only brought him images of the "thousands and tens of thousands who have given up their souls to mammon."[55]

During the last years of the Civil War, what historian Mark Grimsley calls "hard war" came to the South as Union commanders increasingly permitted their men to engage in acts of destruction against Confederate civilians. This strategy, first put into practice in the West in 1863 (later in the East), intended to erode the South's ability to wage war effectively by eliminating its factories, railroads, productive farms, wealth, and cities.[56] It worked quite well. As hard war tactics spread across the western and eastern theaters, southerners wrote increasingly of environmental catastrophe, of finding roads clogged with dead horses, disturbed graves, and torn and burned fields; they watched soldiers kill or take their livestock, loot and destroy their homes, and reduce their important cities to mounds of smoldering rubble.

Excellent firsthand accounts of the devastation wreaked by the war are plentiful, but one of the most striking comes from a selection in Richard Harwell's *The Confederate Reader: How The South Saw the War*. In his section about 1865, Harwell included part of William Gilmore Simms's account of the burning of Columbia, South Carolina. Simms described the event as if Hell itself had erupted on Earth. "Here was Aetna," he wrote, "sending up its spouts of flaming lava; Vesuvius, emulous of like display, shooting up with loftier torrents, and Stromboli, struggling, with awful throes, to shame both by its superior volumes of fluid flame." "The winds," Simms continued, "were tributary to these convulsive efforts and tossed the volcanic torrents hundreds of feet in the air. Great spouts of flame spread aloft in canopies of sulfurous cloud

... edged with sheeted lightnings . . ." A gloom descended upon many regions of the South as northerners made good on threats to "starve, drown, burn, shoot the traitors."[57]

Faced with such calamities, some orators so increasingly disparaged their surroundings that it might be said they were engaging in a celebration of destruction. Benjamin Hill, in March, 1865, described the South's "balmy" climate, fruitful soil, flowing rivers, and land "flowing with milk and with honey," but then devalued this image by asking, "What will it be to us that our skies are bright and our climate balmy, if the spirits of our people are bowed and broken?" He concluded that natural beauty might have to be sacrificed for the war effort. Rather than let Northerners occupy and enjoy the South, he said, "I could pray that God would curse these lands until not a seed could vegetate, and darken these skies until not a ray of light could penetrate the blackness!"[58]

J. Randolph Tucker, speaking at a mass rally in Richmond in February, 1865, apparently agreed. ". . . We must suffer in this contest," he stated, ". . . our houses must be burnt and our fields devastated." Tucker even cast physical destruction as a badge of honor; referring to the despoiled Shenandoah Valley, he described its devastation as a noble wound of war, as a sacrifice worthy of praise rather than sorrow. "Look at the Valley. I am proud of the Valley." He cried. "I have the honor of being born in the valley—which has been devastated from one end to the other." He honored its citizens for refusing to surrender and added "patriotism is like the bruised flower, whose fragrance is but the sweeter for being pressed out upon the breeze."[59]

Rhetorical analysis indicates, therefore, that during the Civil War Confederates experienced a profound change in their attitudes about the environment. In 1861, they had celebrated the beauty and plenty in their surroundings. However, when faced with the destructive effects of military conflict, they were abruptly forced to reconsider their beliefs, to temper their idealized concept of their environment. Audiences still appreciated references to "bright, smiling prairie homes," to sunny skies, mountains, and fertile fields. But, by the end of the war, they also heard that many of their hopes, like much of their region, had become "cruelly blighted, 'like Dead Sea fruits, Which turn to ashes on the lips.'"[60] "Do you love your property?" asked Howell Cobb in 1864, "It has been destroyed and trampled under foot."[61] In other words, the Civil War forced southerners to exchange an idealized portrait of their environment for one that reflected the grim realities of war.

Notes

1 Some interesting statements about the decline of enthusiasm appear in the letters of Dent Confederate Collection, Archives and Manuscripts Department, Auburn University Library, Auburn, Alabama, December 7, 1861.

2 C. Vann Woodward, ed. *Mary Chestnut's Civil War* (New Haven and London: Yale University Press, 1981), 160.

3 Michael Leff, "Topical Invention and Metaphoric Interaction," *Southern Speech Communication Journal*, 48 (Spring, 1983), 214–29, 215. In "A Symposium: The Power of the Symbol," Michael Osborn, Compiler.

4 *Ibid.*, Leff's discussion of the origins and development of interaction theory appears on pages 216–19.

5 *Ibid.*, 217. It should be noted that among rhetoricians Leff has participated extensively in dialogues about the nature of rhetorical criticism and about whether elements of argument and style should be considered separately or integrated into an analysis. He suggests rhetorical critics recognize that functional similarities often exist between form and style, and, as he and Andrew Sachs stated in 1990, that many a discourse blends "form and meaning." Michael Leff, and Andrew Sachs, "Words the Most Like Things: Iconicity and the Rhetorical Text," *Western Journal of Speech Communication* 54 (Summer 1990), 252–73, 270.

6 *Ibid.*, 217, 219.

7   Reverend L. Muller, Sermon at Institute Hall, on Fast Day, June 13, 1861, Delivered Before the German Military Companies and German Population, in *Charleston Daily Courier*, June 17, 1861; J[ames] M[urray] Mason, Speech at Richmond, Virginia, delivered June 8, 1861, in *Echoes from the South, Comprising the Most Important Speeches, Proclamations, and Public Acts Emanating from the South during the Late War* (New York: E. B. Treat & Co., 1866), 172.

8   John Parks, *Sermon before Brigadier-General Hoke's Brigade Upon the Execution of 22 men for Desertion, 28 February, 1864, at Kingston, North Carolina*, (Greensborough, NC: A W. Lincoln & Co., Book and Job Printers, 1864), 6.

9   [Thomas] Watts, Synopsis of remarks before the Mass Meeting, held in Montgomery on February 25, 1865, in *Montgomery Daily Advertiser*, March 3, 1865

10 Bertram Wyatt-Brown, *Southern Honor: Ethics and Behavior in the Old South* (New York and Oxford: Oxford University Press, 1982), 178.

11 William W. Freehling, *The Road To Disunion: Secessionists at Bay, 1776-1854*, vol. 1 (New York and Oxford: Oxford University Press, 1990), 27.

12 John Hope Franklin, *A Southern Odyssey: Travelers in the Antebellum North* (Baton Rouge and London: Louisiana State University Press, 1976), 169.

13 David Golightly Harris, *Piedmont Farmer: The Journals of David Golightly Harris, 1855–1870*, ed. Philip N. Racine (Knoxville: The University of Tennessee Press, 1990), 2.

14 *Ibid.*, 80, 81, 146.

15 *Memphis Daily Appeal*, January 11, 1857.

16 John Pendleton Kennedy, *Swallow Barn; or, A Sojourn in the Old Dominion*, The Library of Southern Civilization (New York: G. P. Putnam & Company, 1853; reprint, Baton Rouge: Louisiana State University Press, 1986), 28–29.

17 Jan Bakker, *Pastoral in Antebellum Southern Romance*, Southern Literary Studies (Baton Rouge and London: Louisiana State University Press, 1989), 1, 58. Readers should note Bakker's argument that antebellum southern romances often tinged pastoral imagery with tragedy or sorrow. Bakker indicates that the pastoral was not intended to generate feelings of bliss, but a sense of loss over man's inability to find true paradise.

18 For an example of a visitor astonished at the rough appearance of the antebellum South, see James Stirling, *Letters from the Slave States* (London: John W Parker and Son, West Strand, 1857), 177. On February 4, 1857, Stirling wrote that the Georgia countryside "is nowhere well cleared; . . . An Englishman, accustomed to clear fields, trim hedge-rows, and regular plantations, can hardly conceive the condition of a Southern State. . . . The cleared portion of the country is trifling compared with that which is yet unreclaimed . . ."

19 Albert E. Cowdrey, *This Land, This South: An Environmental History*, New Perspectives on the South Series, ed. Charles P. Roland (Lexington: The University Press of Kentucky, 1983), 3.

20 Harris, 148.

21 Drew Gilpin Faust, *Southern Stories: Slaveholders in Peace and War* (Columbia, MO and London: University of Missouri Press, 1992), 33, quoting *Southern Agriculturist* 6 (March, 1833).

22 Master Silas Bunch, Address Delivered at the Anniversary of the Charleston Orphan House, Charleston, South Carolina, October 18, 1861, in *Charleston Mercury*, November 15, 1861.

23 A. M. Randolph, *Address on the Day of Fasting and Prayer Appointed by the President of the Confederate States, June 13, 1861, Delivered in St. George's Church, Fredericksburg, Virginia* (Fredericksburg: The Recorder Job Office, 1861), 10; Reverend L. Muller, Sermon at Institute Hall, on Fast Day . . . , in *Charleston Daily Courier*, June 17, 1861; Hon. A. W. Terrell, *Speech Delivered on the 17th January, 1862 in the Representative Hall, Austin, Texas* (Austin: John Marshall & Co., 1862), 28; Mr. Lining, Speech at Fourth of July Celebration, July 4, 1861, Charleston, South Carolina, in *Charleston Daily Courier*, July 6, 1861.

24 Mr. Samuel L. Hammond, Speech at Fourth of July Celebration, in *Charleston Daily Courier*, July 6, 1861.

25 Bunch, October 18, 1861.

26 Reverend E. T. Winkler, *Duties of the Citizen Soldier. A Sermon Delivered in the First Baptist Church of Charleston, S.C., on Sabbath Morning, January 6, 1861, before the Moultrie Guards. By E. T. Winkler, Chaplain of the Company* (Charleston: A. J. Burke, 1861), 1; Rt. Reverend Stephen Elliott, *Our Cause in Harmony with the Purposes of God in Christ Jesus. A Sermon Preached in Christ Church, Savannah, on Thursday September 18, 1862, Being the Day*

Set Forth by the President of the Confederate States, as a Day of Prayer and Thanksgiving, for our Manifold Victories, and Especially for the Fields of Manassas and Richmond, Ky. (Savannah: Power Press of John M. Cooper & Co., 1862), 9; Bunch.

27 Hon. Thos. J. Devine, *Speech Delivered on the 17th January, 1862, in the Representative Hall, Austin, Texas* (Austin: John Marshall & Co., 1862), 8–9.

28 Speakers, for example, often used definition to explain the boundaries of their country. See Alexander Stephens, Speech Delivered on the 21st March, 1861, in Savannah, Known as "The Corner Stone Speech," Reported in the *Savannah Republican*, in Henry Cleveland, *Alexander Stephens in Public and Private. With Letters and Speeches before, during, and since the War* (Philadelphia: National Publishing Co., 1866), 723-724. "In extent of territory," Stephens claimed, "we embrace five hundred and sixty-four thousand square miles and upward. This is upward of two hundred thousand square miles more than was included within the limits of the original thirteen States." Likewise, see T[homas] R. R. Cobb, Substance of an Address of T. R. R. Cobb to his Constituents of Clark County, location unknown, April 6, 1861 (n. p.), 2. Cobb asked, "Who now are our confederates? . . . Alabama and Mississippi, Georgia's twin daughters, whose sons [sic] great souls partake of the boundlessness of their fertile plains, and the outpouring freedom of the mighty river which washes their western limits. Louisiana, with a history as pure and an escutcheon as spotless as the white breasted [sic] bird which floats upon her banner. And last, . . . Texas, with her forest sons . . ."

29 Daniel Baringer, Address on the importance of an agricultural education, extract, location unknown, date unknown, in *Milledgeville Federal Union*, April 16, 1861.

30 Howell Cobb, Speech at Atlanta, delivered May 29(?), 1861, in *Milledgeville Federal Union*, June 4, 1861

31 For an example of an orator linking natural beauty to the divine, see Reverend J. Gierlow, Sermon: A View of the Present Crisis, Baton Rouge, Louisiana, August, 1861 (n. p., n. d.) source unknown, 4. Gierlow said, "He keeps the ocean sweet with the breath of His tempests, and He purifies the stagnant atmosphere with the fire of His forked lightenings."

32 Charles W. Russell, Address Before the Richmond Medical College, date unknown, in *Richmond Enquirer*, March 28, 1862.

33 *Aiken, South Carolina: A Description of the Climate, Soils, and the Nature of the Products in the Vicinity of Aiken, South Carolina, Especially Fruit, Cereals, Cotton, Corn, etc Including Extracts from Letters of Distinguished Visitors, Correspondents, Action of Town Councils Inviting Emigrants, etc., etc.* (New York: J. C. Derby, Pub., 1870), 21.

34 Richard Yeadon, The Garden and the Vineyard, Anniversary Address Before the Aiken Vine-Growing and Horticultural Association, date unknown, in *Charleston Daily Courier*, August 30, 1862.

35 *Milledgeville Federal Union*, June 4, 1861

36 John A. Gilmer, Speech of Honorable John A. Gilmer, of North Carolina, in the United States House of Representatives, January 26, 1861. In *Hillsborough Recorder*, February 13, 1861.

37 H. N. Pierce, *Sermons Preached in St. John's Church, Mobile, Alabama, on the 13th of June, 1861, The National Fast, Appointed by His Excellency Jefferson Davis, President of the Confederate States of America* (Mobile: Farrow & Dennett, Book and Job Printers, 1861), 4.

38 For a speaker hinting at future difficulties, see Howell Cobb, Speech at Atlanta, Georgia, May 22, 1861, in *Echoes from the South*, 183. Cobb warned that Virginia's "soil is to be the battle ground, and her streams are to be dyed with southern blood." See also Henry Wise, Jefferson Davis, Speeches at Public Meeting, location and date obscured [Richmond, June 1, 1861], in *Milledgeville Federal Union*, June 11, 1861. Wise predicted that southerners would have to face "flame and smoke, or . . . a river of blood," while Jefferson Davis suggested that the South was threatened by a "tide of . . . despotism." The Reverend J. Gierlow also spoke on the subject. Gierlow, Sermon in August, 1861, 5. Gierlow added that, like Hercules, though the South had "throttled the serpents that were sent to strangle him . . . there are also Lernean hydras yet to be destroyed . . . before the golden fruit in the garden of the Hesperides can be gathered."

39 Charles W. Russell, Address before the Richmond Medical College, date unknown, in *Richmond Enquirer*, March 28, 1862.

40 C. Sidney Lobdell, Speech at the Flag Presentation to the Delta Rifles, Baton Rouge, Louisiana, April 20, 1861, in *West Baton Rouge Sugar Planter*, April 27, 1861.

41 Richard B. Harwell, ed., *The Confederate Reader: How the South Saw the War* (New York: Longmans, Green and Co., Inc., 1957; New York: Dover Publications, Inc., 1989), 144, quoting *Southern Illustrated News*.

42 John T. Trowbridge, *The Desolate South, 1865–1866: A Picture of the Battlefields and of the Devastated Confederacy*, ed. Gordon Carroll (New York: Duell, Sloan and Pearce, c 1956), 81.

43 Governor Zebulon Vance, Inaugural Address, delivered in Raleigh, North Carolina, September 8, 1862, in *Wilmington Journal Weekly*, September 18, 1862.

44 William Yancey, Speech on retaliation, delivered in the Confederate Senate, August 21, 1862 (n. p., n. d.), 7.

45 Benjamin H. Hill, Speech Delivered Before the Georgia Legislature, in Milledgeville, December 11, 1862, in Benjamin H. Hill, Jr., *Senator Benjamin H. Hill of Georgia, His Life, Speeches, and Writings* (Atlanta: T. H. P. Bloodworth, 1893), 254, 271.

46 Williamson Oldham, Speech of W. S. Oldham, of Texas, upon the Bill to Amend the Conscript Law, made in the Confederate Senate, September 4, 1862, (n. p.), 8.

47 James Phelan, Speech of Hon. James Phelan of Mississippi on the Judiciary Bill, delivered in the Confederate Senate, exact date unknown, 1862? (n. p.), 11, 12.

48 W. G. Swan, *Foreign Relations. Speech of Hon. W. G. Swan, of Tennessee, Delivered in the House of Representatives of the Confederate States, February 5, 1863* (Richmond: Smith, Bailey & Co., Printers, 1863), 6.

49 Governor Zebulon Vance, Speech on Washington's Birthday, delivered to the citizens of Wilkes County, at Hillsborough(?), North Carolina, February 22, 1864. In *Hillsborough Recorder*, March 9, 1864; Reverend D. S. Doggett, *The War and Its Close. A Discourse Delivered in Centenary Church, Richmond, Va., Friday, April 8, 1864, on the Occasion of the National Fast* (Richmond: Macfarlane & Ferguson, 1864), 10.

50 Muller, Sermon at Institute Hall.

51 Brigadier-General E. W. Gantt, C. S. A., *Address* (Little Rock: publisher not named, 1863), in University Archives, Howard-Tilton Memorial Library, Tulane University, New Orleans, Louisiana, 19.

52 Mr. Perkins, Remarks of Mr. Perkins, of Louisiana, in the Confederate House of Representatives, May 3, 1864 (n. p.), 4.

53 W. T. D. Dalzell, *Thanksgiving to God. A Sermon Preached in St. Mark's Church, San Antonio, on Wednesday, 4th February, 1863* (San Antonio: Herald Book and Job Press, n. d.), 8; Rev. I. R. Finley, *The Lord Reigneth: A Sermon Preached in Lloyd's Church, Sussex County, Va., Sunday, August 16, 1863* (Richmond: Chas. H. Wynne, Printer, n. d.), 12; Rt. Rev. Stephen Elliott, *"Vain is the Help of Man." A Sermon Preached in Christ Church, Savannah, on Thursday, September 15, 1864, Being the Day of Fasting, Humiliation, and Prayer, Appointed by the Governor of the State of Georgia* (Macon, GA: Burke, Boykin & Company, 1864), 6, 10.

54 Gantt, *Address*, 12, 11, 18.

55 A[lbert] G[allatin] Brown, State of the Country. Speech of Hon. A. G. Brown of Mississippi, delivered in the Confederate Senate, December 24, 1863, (n. p.), 2.

56 Mark Grimsley, *The Hard Hand of War: Union Military Policy toward Southern Civilians, 1861–1865* (Cambridge: Cambridge University Press, 1995).

57 Richard B. Harwell, ed., *The Confederate Reader*, 356–57; Charles Royster, *The Destructive War: William Tecumseh Sherman, Stonewall Jackson and the Americans* (New York: Alfred A. Knopf, 1991; New York: Vintage Civil War Library, Vintage Books, 1993), 80, quoting Judge Levi Hubbell, April, 1861; Additional accounts of how the Civil War affected the southern environment can be found in Stephen V. Ash's *When the Yankees Came: Conflict and Chaos in the Occupied South, 1861–1865* (Chapel Hill and London: University of North Carolina Press, 1995).

58 Benjamin H. Hill, Speech delivered at La Grange, GA, March 11, 1865, in *Senator Benjamin H. Hill of Georgia, His Life, Speeches, and Writings*, 274–75.

59 J. Randolph Tucker, Speech at the mass meeting at the African Church, February 9, 1865, in *Richmond Enquirer*, February 13, 1865. For additional examples of speakers who seem to celebrate destruction, see Rt. Rev. Stephen Elliott, *Vain is the Help of Man*, 1864, 5–6. At one point in this sermon, Elliott stated, "Were we to come out of this conflict, alone of all the States, rich, unharmed, undevastated, we should come out without a local history, without any thing for tradition to hang glory upon, without those scars of honor which designate the veteran hero. . . . Better for us, as a State, that we should bear our portion of the general suffering . . ."

Elliott even argued that "our fields may be sown with blood and desolation, but the harvest may be one of national character which shall bless us for long generations."

One of the most dramatic examples of this tendency to emphasize destruction can be found in a post-war sermon. In 1865, the Reverend J. L. Blitch raised the denigration of the environment to new levels. Blitch referred to the "gory fields of carnage" produced by war and subsequently launched into a bitter denunciation of the natural environment. "Time and disease," he said, "destroy our fondest anticipations and blast our most flattering prospects. Death unrelentingly severs the tenderest ties of earth, while the cankering worm makes carnival of the dissolving body. . . . Decay is written indelibly on every thing before our vision. The flower, early and flush with the morning dews, has pencilled in its delicate leaves destruction." He added, "That mountain, whose antiquated peaks reach the distant skies, and against which the furious storms and rapid tempests have often beaten with vehemence, shall crumble to dust." Reverend J. L. Blitch, *"Thy Kingdom Come." A Sermon Preached to the Aberdeen Church by their Pastor* (Augusta, GA: The Baptist Banner Press, 1865), 3, 5.

60 Williamson Oldham, Speech of Hon. W. S. Oldham, of Texas, on the Resolutions of the State of Texas, concerning Peace, Reconstruction, and Independence, delivered in the Confederate Senate, January 30, 1865, (n. p.), In Center for American History, The University of Texas at Austin, 3, 8.

61 Howell Cobb, Speech at Atlanta, January 28, 1864, in Frank Moore, ed, *The Rebellion Record: A Diary of American Events, with Documents, Narratives, Illustrative Incidents, Poetry, etc.*, Vol. 8 (New York: D. Van Nostrand, 1867), 342.

CHAPTER FIVE

Slavery and Slaves:
A Growing Unease

THOUGH DESCRIPTIONS of the South's landscape and natural phenomena occurred frequently in Confederate oratory, the resulting environmental portrait often contained a striking omission. It lacked inhabitants, for in many cases orators neglected to include a human presence in the "fields . . . clothed with the rich glories of the harvest" or to acknowledge the role men played in developing the region's natural features. Furthermore, on those occasions when they mentioned human handiwork, speakers often employed generic, unspecific language. In the rhetoric of Alexander Stephens, for example, "we" often sufficed to explain who "dug down the hills, and filled up the valleys."[1] In another case, a speaker referred to unspecified "laborers" who would harness the waterfalls of North Carolina.[2]

In Confederate rhetoric, therefore, millions of white cultivators and an estimated four million slaves received, in contrast to the natural environment, rather perfunctory treatment. Though not ignored, slaves were handled inconsistently; sometimes addressed in detail, but as often subject to oblique reference or oddly excluded from relevant discussion. And given the significance of slavery in the antebellum South and in the creation of the Confederacy, that bondsmen and the institution under which they labored were not afforded greater rhetorical prominence seems particularly remarkable.

Historians agree that antebellum slavery had tremendous, far-reaching effects on the South, that its influence, as Kenneth Greenburg has written, "seemed to echo endlessly through all areas of Southern thought and behavior."[3] According to William Cooper, Jr., it was the central issue of antebellum politics, permeating not only the rhetoric of southern statesmen, but shaping their political battles into contests over its defense.[4] And, Greenburg adds, because many politicians were slaveowners, the institution also affected their style of statesmanship. In office, many behaved in a manner reminiscent of that of a master, at once authoritarian, independent, concerned, and just.[5]

The influence of slavery has also been noted in some of the South's most distinctive social characteristics. The region did not experience widespread industrial development, for example, in part because many southerners believed that slaves could not work effectively in a factory setting. Fears that slaves could not be controlled in an urban environment helped to slow the growth of southern cities. And whites, confronted daily with the effects of enslavement, developed a distinctive and passionate devotion to freedom, a passion they curiously paired with a powerful desire to maintain black slavery at all costs. Though only about one quarter of all southerners owned slaves, whites nevertheless united behind the institution, whether because it conferred a degree of superiority on even the lowliest of their race, or because most aspired to ownership. Southerners bought slaves to display their prosperity and achievements. As one Union officer noticed from his Civil War post in Tennessee, "All of the people who had obtained any sort of success . . . had owned slaves."[6]

But slavery's greatest effect on the antebellum South may lie in its role in secession and in the creation of the Confederacy, for the events of early 1861 were rooted in decades of disagreement over the nature of the institution, its future, and its place in the Union. From 1830 to 1860, in conflict over territorial rights, and faced with accusations of immorality in their slaveownership, southerners responded by developing what one historian calls a "systematic and self-conscious" proslavery ideology.[7] In so doing, they came to focus increasingly on slavery as they approached the 1860s.

Southerners constructed the ideology from foundations established in the eighteenth century. They reiterated the regionally-accepted notion that slavery operated under divine approval, but added historical and scientific data as additional supports. They also appended a humanitarian element aimed directly at free labor activists, an argument that slavery actually benefited the bondsman by showering him with more advantages and kindness than he could expect as a free worker. And, southerners explained in detail the benefits that slavery offered the nation, noting how slave labor enabled the South to produce tremendous numbers of food crops. During the antebellum period, as the South faced increasing opposition to the institution, this ideology came to occupy not only the contents of its speeches, sermons, and lectures, but also the pages of its novels and lines of its poetry. Citizens confirmed the salience of slavery in their lives by ordering some twenty-five thousand copies of James Henry Hammond's 1858 "Mud-Sill" speech and leading Edmund Ruffin to remark, in 1859, that his most recent slavery pamphlet had attracted more notice "than . . . anything I ever wrote before."[8]

The South, therefore, faced the divisive issues of 1859 and 1860 with a strong proslavery attitude and a strong desire to defend the institution. In late 1860 and early 1861, this mentality translated into action as fears generated by the election of Abraham Lincoln, a man condemned by one speaker specifically for "his hatred of slavery," prompted the lower South to leave the Union.[9] The New Orleans *Bee* explained the significance of the institution to disunion. "As long as slavery is looked upon by the North with abhorrence," read one editorial, "as long as the South is regarded as a mere slave-breeding and slave-driving community; as long as false and pernicious theories are cherished respecting inherent equality . . . there can be no satisfactory political union between the two sections."[10]

Given the intensity of proslavery feeling present at the birth of the Confederacy, one might expect the rhetoric of the new nation to have dealt directly and extensively with the institution, to have deliberated its role in the independent South, and to have openly and consistently mentioned slaves. Surprisingly, though, this is not quite what happened. In Confederate rhetoric, lengthy treatments of slavery or slaves appeared less often than might be expected, generally only in association with a handful of specific issues, and in certain types of orations. Congressional debates did include reference to slaves and did encompass the management of the institution and its contributions to the Confederacy. A number of sermons also referred to slavery at length. An examination of the popular oratory, however, including the sermons to soldiers, the speeches at rallies, farewell orations, graduation addresses, and the published snippets from conventions and legislative debates, indicates that on numerous occasions the institution and its bondsmen were treated with far more brevity. With a few exceptions, extensive discussions were limited to the beginning of the Civil War, as Confederates sought to unify, and to the end, as they debated arming slaves against the North. In the intervening years, references to both the institution and its bondsmen noticeably declined.

Still, more than enough words were spoken to support analysis and to reveal something of how Confederates conceived of slavery and slaves. Civil War southerners, it seems, harbored a complex array of feelings toward both. Their rhetoric does include instances of praise for slave labor and for the individuals in bondage, as well as moments in which speakers voiced antebellum proslavery arguments. In January, 1861, the Reverend W. H. Watkins of Natchez, Mississippi, delivered an extremely charitable portrait of slavery in which he acknowledged its role in developing the South. "African slavery," he said, ". . . has done more for civilization, commerce, wealth, and the uplifting of human society, than any other political institution known to man." God, Watkins concluded, made slavery "a blessing to mankind."[11] South Carolina Governor Pickens, celebrating the fall of Fort Sumter in April, also praised slavery as "a source of strength in war," while, in 1864, Henry Watkins Allen stated that "this institution will triumph with us, because it is right and just in the sight of Almighty God."[12] Even as the Confederacy crumbled in March, 1865, Benjamin Hill of Georgia still insisted that slavery was vital to the well-being of the black American. "Slavery," he stated, "is the only civilizer of the negro [sic]."[13]

Praise for slaves appears in Confederate rhetoric as well. Speakers variously referred to slaves as members of a "most affectionate race," as "well-bred courteous" individuals, and as friends. They spoke of slaves as a "source of wealth incalculable," as one of the "unmistakable elements of a great nation," and as "civilized, hardy and happy laborers," who "made the wilderness a garden" and "enrich[ed] the civilized world."[14] Even in September, 1864, one finds speakers talking about the obedience of slaves and pointing out that "Their quiet has been wonderful even to ourselves, and has caused the world . . . to wonder."[15]

No oratory, though, approaches the level of praise extended by the Reverend C. C. Jones in December, 1861. Speaking to a Georgia audience, Jones defined bondsmen as the allies of their masters, stating that "they are not enemies but friends; they are not foreigners, but our nearest neighbors; they are not hired servants, but servants belonging to us in law and gospel; born in our house, and bought with our money . . ."[16] He described a fundamentally close link between master and slave by pointing out that white children were nursed at the "generous breasts" of slaves, and that "among the last forms that our failing eyes do see, and among the last sounds our ears do hear, are their forms and their weepings, mingled with those of our dearest ones, as they bend over us in our last struggles, dying . . ."[17] Jones also spoke directly to the contributions slaves made as producers, for he pointed out that "the immense returns of our soil come from their patient labors. . . . They were the mainspring, the mighty power that set and kept in motion, year after year, the unexampled and ever increasing wealth and prosperity of the whole country."[18]

Reading these and other words, one might assume that southerners maintained their proslavery mentality throughout the Civil War. A thorough examination of Confederate rhetoric, however, reveals that Civil War southerners were actually inconsistent in their attitudes towards slavery and slaves. Evidence that Confederates had certain reservations about slavery appears in their rhetoric as early as Spring, 1861. In this first year, orators spoke directly and favorably about the institution fairly often. Direct references, however, constituted only one of the rhetorical means through which slavery appeared, for speakers also alluded to the subject by weaving its terminology into their discourse, using words and phrases associated with the institution to

describe subjects as varied as the economy, the North, and conscription. In this behavior, one finds that slavery almost always
had negative connotations. Orators unerringly joined slave terminology to subjects they felt could be harmful and should be
avoided, and so associated slavery with trouble, problems, and
disorder.

Indirect references to slavery took many forms. For example,
the physical objects and instruments used in controlling the slave
population were often mentioned in reference to the North. The
Reverend L. Muller, in a June, 1861 sermon before German military companies, described northern aggression in terms of slave
catching, noting the North had turned loose "bloodhounds" on the
South "to blot our honor and annihilate our existence." The northern press, he added, the "vile slave of their brutal pubic opinion,"
applauded.[19] Other speakers condemned Yankees for attempting
"to play master" in southern households, for seeking to "chain the
hands and close the mouths" of southern citizens, and for "lift[ing]
the threatened lash of Coercion."[20] This tendency to join slavery
terms with the North continued through the war. In September,
1862, for example, W. E. Simms referred in the Confederate Senate
to the "enslaved and subsidised press of the North," while Dr.
Palmer of South Carolina echoed earlier speakers when he told an
audience of soldiers that "For three years we have held the bloodhounds at bay."[21] A military chaplain told soldiers in Virginia that
the North intended to place "manacles of despotism" upon southerners, and Williamson Oldham predicted in January, 1865, that
the North would interpret Confederate peace overtures as evidence that southerners were "at last ready to submit and bow our
necks to the yoke."[22]

As the war continued, negative imagery began increasingly to
cloud direct statements about slavery as well. The year 1863 found
E. W. Gantt of Arkansas referring to slavery as a "cankering sore."[23]

In a January congressional oration, John Baldwin of Virginia noted that slavery actually harmed the southern war effort. Because the Confederacy was "founded upon the institution of slavery," he said, . . . "the sympathies of the world were against us."[24] Even the Reverend Stephen Elliott, who spent pages in an 1862 sermon discussing how slavery was a "divinely guarded system, planted by God, protected by God, and arranged for his own wise purposes," also felt the need to warn in this same oration that the institution could at any time become "pricks in our eyes and thorns in our sides, and . . . vex us in the land wherein we dwell."[25] By 1863, Elliott was starting to speak of slavery in even harsher terms, stating that the "curse of God upon sin, . . . manifested itself in poverty, in suffering, in slavery . . ."[26]

An examination of the words spoken about slaves uncovers a similar inconsistency of thought, though one slightly more dramatic than that voiced in regard to slavery. Indeed, analysis indicates that, during the course of the Civil War speakers increasingly began altering slaves from happy laborers into savage enemies capable of "burn[ing] your home and murder[ing] you and your families."[27] Some denigrated bondsmen to the point that they were rendered valueless. One Virginia state senator called blacks "inferior in their mental faculties, and so inferior as to be incapable of the sustained effort and the sedulous toil."[28] The Reverend Elliott agreed that slaves were not desirable and used a particularly powerful form of argument–anaphora–to make this point. "These slaves," he said, "*were imposed upon us–imposed upon us,* in many cases against our wills–*imposed upon us* just so long as it was profitable for those hypocrites to bring them here."[29][emphasis added] In 1865, speakers variously described slaves as "flat-nosed, thick-lipped sons of Africa," "Naturally averse to labor" and expert thieves.[30]

In addition, actions specifically associated with slaves were joined to behaviors southerners wanted to discourage. Governor

Vance warned citizens that "slavish subservience to those in power . . . injures both giver and recipient, [and] is to be avoided and despised."[31] Condemning the problems of desertion, one man said that runaway soldiers "[took] to the woods," thereby applying to them an expression antebellum masters reserved for runaway slaves.[32] And black slaves were described as tools of the North intended to take over the South, enslave white men, and assault white women. In January, 1864, Governor Allen warned that Louisiana blacks were already starting to experiment with powers granted to them by northern forces. During his inaugural address, he noted that one of the great outrages of "Butler the Beast" involved his accepting the "false accusation of a negro [sic] woman" as an excuse for dragging from a sick bed one of the "most respectable citizens of New Orleans" and throwing him in jail.[33] Likewise, Governor Vance described the "dreadful" happenings in Beaufort, South Carolina. Whites had been expelled from this town, Vance noted, and its lands put up for sale. "Colored men," he said, "are the principal buyers," resulting in "Your lands confiscated and sold to your own slaves!"[34]

Given that speakers seek to orate the beliefs of their listeners, this information suggests that, in regard to black slaves, southerners did not sustain a proslavery argument during the Civil War. Indeed, judging from comments made in 1864 and 1865, some seem to have turned on the institution and on slaves. And faced with the basic question of why such a transformation took place, one finds insight by returning to this chapter's original observation. It has been suggested that Confederate orators treated slaves and slavery in a rather cursory manner, often leaving these subjects out of relevant speeches or handling them with brevity. A detailed study of their absence indicates that this oversight was calculated, that southerners, in defining and creating their new nation, failed to consistently outline a province for slavery or for slaves.

Throughout the conflict, orators carefully segregated the Confederacy, clearly indicating that certain areas were the rhetorical domain of whites alone. Slaves, for example, were at first not even remotely associated with the military. Instructing soldiers in the sacred trappings of their country, speakers cast homes, firesides, liberty, soil, and honor as worthy of defense, but completely ignored slaves and slavery. Nor did they include a slave presence in depictions of soldiers' loved ones. In Confederate oratory, as Howell Cobb made very clear in 1864, the military family did not admit blacks. Arguing that Georgians should care and provide for soldiers' families, he twice made certain his audience understood exactly whom he meant: "When I see a soldier's wife whose little ones are dependent upon her labor for support . . . I am compelled in my heart to say there is some great wrong somewhere. . . . See to it that no soldier's wife or child shall suffer."[35] Nathaniel Boyden of North Carolina similarly limited the family. Describing conscription in 1864, he noted its terrible effects on southerners, how it "enter[ed] the dwelling of the poor widow, whose father and husband have fallen in battle; it finds there the one son of the military age and a number of helpless and dependent daughters. The son is the only one upon the farm capable of following the plowshare and is the whole stay and support of the family . . ."[36]

Faced with proposals to draft slaves into the Confederate army in 1864, a number of orators responded forcefully, arguing at length that such actions would not only destroy the South's military might, but also ruin the institution as well. Many expressed horror at the idea of blacks serving alongside white soldiers. Thomas Gholson of Virginia, a lawyer and judge before the war, pointed out through a precisely-ordered speech that "Our soldiers have been brought up to believe . . . the negro [sic] an inferior race. Will they then consent to march and fight with this inferior race, on terms of equality?"[37] H. C. Chambers believed the answer would always be the negative, claiming "Even victory itself would be robbed of its glory if shared with slaves."[38]

Even those orators who advocated placing slaves in the military did so with a certain resignation. They pointedly refrained from describing blacks as gallant or courageous, stating that the strength of armed slaves lay merely in their numbers and endurance. And several orators noted that the idea of black soldiers originated in the North. Gustavus Henry, speaking in Richmond in February, 1865, captured the mood voiced by several slave advocates, first stating forcefully that "I shall not hesitate about bringing him [the slave] forward," but flippantly adding "Why not? Don't he fight on the other side by compulsion? Certainly he does, and he will also fight on our side."[39] Similarly, Judah P. Benjamin pointed out that "Every one knew that the Yankees had told the negro [sic] if he would come and fight for them they would make them free; it was now for us to stop him from going to the Yankees."[40]

The rhetoric from both sides of this issue indicates that slaves were not welcome as full and honored members of the Confederate army, a circumstance that does not seem surprising in light of how orators defined and described their military. The southern fighting man, according to many a speaker, had an abundance of courage, a sense of personal honor, and a strong determination to defend his nation's rights. He was moral, temperate, and merciful, but also steeled to the tasks of war. A South Carolinian called soldiers the "flower, and the hope and the pride" of their communities, while the Reverend John Parks concluded that *"Such men as these were never born to be slaves."*[41]

Soldiers, it seems, were so far removed from slavery they were not even permitted to fight for its defense. When Confederate speakers listed the individuals and objects for which southern men fought, they generally listed friends, family, homes, land, girlfriends, and children, but not slaves or slavery. This is true in speeches from 1861 as well as those from 1865. In July, 1861, a speaker told a Virginia audience that southerners were "fighting for the dearest, most precious gifts of earth—just government, native soil, life, homes, wives, children."[42] Similarly, an orator in 1865 argued that the South fought to "defend their altars and their homes, the lives and honour of their wives and children."[43]

But just as speakers did not associate slaves with the Confederate military, they also failed, in many cases, to define a role for their bondsmen in the civilian war effort. There were occasions, especially in Congressional debate, in which slaves were included in the war effort and their role acknowledged. However, there were also surprising instances in which they were pointedly ignored. In Congress, for example, debate on the proposed burning of cotton and tobacco, both crops strongly associated with slave labor, often ignored the institution. Henry Foote of Mississippi, speaking sarcastically against the proposal, indicated that destruction would be carried out by men like himself. "It is indeed," he said sarcastically, "a great virtue *with one's own hand* to pauperize one's self and family" [emphasis added]. Jabez Curry countered that there was no man in his state of Alabama "so avaricious that he would not, with his own hands, put the torch to every lock of cotton." Speakers fretted over the effects of such devastation, but limited their focus to men and "families." And, though they talked about keeping "useful" properties from the Union army, slaves were not mentioned.[44]

Similarly, in June, 1861, the Reverend H. N. Pierce gave a fast-day sermon which dealt extensively with cotton. He repeatedly spoke of the crop's significance, first yelling "Cotton is King!" and then later acknowledging that this expression "has frequently met my eye in the public prints and saluted my ear upon the thoroughfares . . ." However, at no point did he mention the role of slaves in its production. Speaking of cotton planting, he was vague, merely stating that "we are providentially the producers of an article which is of so much commercial value. . . . Herein we possess a mighty element of national strength." Describing potential agents of cotton's destruction, he again neglected men, listing drought, plague, insects, and flood. Though he spoke at length about a subject eminently related to slavery, he failed to link its fortunes to the institution or its bondsmen.[45]

Some speakers did not include blacks as they praised the Confederacy and spoke of the importance of morals and devotion to God. Orators urged planters to grow food staples and to sell their cotton and rice crops to the government without so much as an allusion to the slaves responsible for the harvest. Slaves almost completely vanished from the political speeches of 1862 and 1863 and did not reappear with any strength until 1864, in controversy over whether to employ black troops in the Confederate army. Again, part of the reason for the exclusion of slaves may lie in the initial definitions of Confederate character. Southern civilians, speakers said initially, "breath[ed] freely the air of Independence . . . and maintain[ed] our claim to manhood."[46] They were patriots, working together with "warm hearts and busy fingers" in the defense of their rights, acting with courage, gallantry, wisdom, and self-respect, and, therefore, nothing like those perceived as simple, inferior slaves.[47]

Analysis also reveals that just as slavery was often segregated from the confederate military and from confederate society, it also had a limited role in Confederate oratory. Indeed, as speakers voiced positive comments, they often relegated the institution into a rhetorical function. Rather than uniformly celebrating or mentioning it for its own merits, as had been the practice before the war, they more often employed slavery as a means of persuasion, attaching it collaterally to another primary issue, or downplayed its value in a speech altogether. Examples of this treatment appear in Robert Smith's 1861 oration on the Confederate Constitution, and in Alexander Stephens's "Cornerstone" speech.

Smith, urging southerners to unite in accepting the Confederate Constitution, cited the document's recognition and protection of slavery as one proof of its efficacy. He talked at some length on the subject, mostly reiterating proslavery arguments–that history sanctioned the institution, and that slavery benevolently transformed the "wild savage" into "a civilized appendage to the family relation." Turning to the Constitution, he noted with pride that "We have now placed our domestic institution, and secured its rights unmistakably, in the Constitution; we have sought by no euphony to hide its name–we have called our negroes 'slaves' . . ." However, Smith downplayed the importance of slavery through his language, stating at one point, "let the subject pass," and at another, "so much for this question of strife."[48] He also buried the issue in the last third of his oration, inserting it just after a discussion of new postal policies, and just before a brief treatment of the policies for admitting states. Slavery, therefore, appeared simply as one of many factors improved by the new document.

Such was also the case in a rather famous oration by Alexander Stephens. On March 21, 1861, Stephens gave what has been called the "Cornerstone" speech in Savannah, Georgia. This particular work has been cited frequently as evidence that slavery was highly important to Confederates, for, at one point, Stephens claimed that the "corner-stone" of the southern nation "rests upon the great truth that the negro [sic] is not equal to the white man; that slavery–subordination to the superior race–is his natural and normal condition."[49]

However, what historians have overlooked in this oration is that it did not primarily concern slavery. Instead, it was partly an analysis of the new Constitution, partly a discussion of southern strengths, and partly a set of optimistic predictions for the South's future, with condemnation of the North added for spite. Slavery was introduced as one of many constitutional issues and presented in a fairly unspectacular manner. Stephens led into the subject weakly, almost apologizing for including it in the oration. "Not to be tedious in enumerating the numerous changes for the better," he said, "allow me to allude to one other—though last, not least."[50] And once grappling with slavery, he simply reiterated accepted information about the divinely-ordained inferiority of the slave, the historical precedent for slavery, and the civilizing influence of the institution. His words did not generate any great applause (as did subsequent statements about southern independence and wisdom) and were not particularly original; to some extent, in fact, he echoed the antebellum rhetoric of James Henry Hammond, who referred to slavery as a "cornerstone" of liberty in the 1850s. In 1858, Hammond equated slaves with "the very mud-sill [class] of society," a statement similar to Stephens's 1861 claim that slaves were the "substratum of our society . . . made of the material fitted by nature for [their position]." Stephens' "cornerstone" statement may have caught the attention of history, but slavery did not constitute the cornerstone of his speech. It was a secondary factor, abruptly dismissed with the curt statement, "But to pass on."[51]

Considering the limitations in the overall rhetorical treatment of slaves and of slavery, it might be said that Southerners voiced inconsistent words about both subjects because they were vulnerable. That Confederate orators neglected to determine a congruous role for slaves to perform in their new country, indicates their audiences did not expect slaves to enjoy full participation in the military or to contribute extensively and consistently on the homefront. Therefore, as the national situation grew more and more perilous by 1864, causing white southerners to turn on each other, it seems understandable that some turned slavery and slaves into the subjects of scorn.

Notes

1   Master Silas Bunch, Address Delivered at the Anniversary of the Charleston Orphan House, Charleston, South Carolina, October 18, 1861, in *Charleston Mercury*, November 15, 1861; Alexander Stephens, Speech in Savannah, Georgia, delivered March 21, 1861, Known as "The Corner Stone Speech," reported in the *Savannah Republican*, in Henry Cleveland, *Alexander Stephens, in Public and Private. With Letters and Speeches before, during, and since the War* (Philadelphia: National Publishing Co., 1866), 719.

2   Samuel Hall, Remarks of the Commissioner from Georgia before the General Assembly of North Carolina, February 13, 1861, in *Wilmington Journal Weekly*, February 14, 1861.

3   Kenneth S. Greenberg, *Masters and Statesmen: The Political Culture of American Slavery* (Baltimore and London: The Johns Hopkins University Press, 1985), ix.

4   William J. Cooper, Jr., *The South and the Politics of Slavery: 1828–1856* (Baton Rouge and London: Louisiana State University Press, 1978).

5   Greenberg, 21.

6   Stephen V. Ash, *Middle Tennessee Society Transformed, 1860–1870: War and Peace in the Upper South* (Baton Rouge and London: Louisiana State University Press, 1988), 44, quoting John Wisner Hinkley, *A Narrative of Service with the Third Wisconsin Infantry* (Madison, 1912), 112.

7   Drew Gilpin Faust, ed., *The Ideology of Slavery: Proslavery Thought in the Antebellum South, 1830–1860* (Baton Rouge: Louisiana State University Press, 1981), 4.

8   For an example of a proslavery advocate describing the benefits of the institution, see E. N. Elliott, *Cotton is King and Pro-Slavery Arguments: Comprising the Writings of Hammond, Harper, Christy, Stringfellow, Hodge, Bledsoe, and Cartwright, on this Important Subject* (Augusta, GA: Pritchard, Abbott & Loomis, 1860). Information on the "Mud-Sill" Speech from Drew Gilpin Faust, *James Henry Hammond and the Old South: A Design for Mastery*

(Baton Rouge and London: Louisiana State University Press, 1982), 347; Faust, ed., *Ideology of Slavery*, 5, quoting Edmund Ruffin, Diary, January 29, 1859.

9   Henry Benning, Speech before the Virginia State Convention, February 14, 1861, in Frank Moore, ed, *The Rebellion Record: A Diary of American Events, with Documents, Narratives, Illustrative Incidents, Poetry, etc.*, Supplement Vol. 1 (New York: D. Van Nostrand, 1866), 148.

10   Kenneth M. Stampp, ed., *The Causes of the Civil War* (New York: Simon & Schuster, Inc., 1986), 114, quoting New Orleans *Bee*, December 14, 1860.

11   W. H. Watkins, The South, Her Position and Duty. A Discourse Delivered at the Methodist Church, Natchez, Mississippi, January 4, 1861, (n. p.), in Mississippi Department Archives and History, Jackson, Mississippi, 5.

12   Governor Francis Pickens, Speech at Charleston, South Carolina, April 14(?), 1861, in *Charleston Courier*, April 15, 1861; Governor Henry Watkins Allen, Inaugural Address of Governor Henry W. Allen, to the Legislature of the State of Louisiana, Delivered at Shreveport, January 25, 1864, (n. p.), in Special Collections, Louisiana State University Libraries, Baton Rouge, Louisiana, 8.

13   Benjamin H. Hill, Speech Delivered at La Grange, Georgia, March 11, 1865, in Benjamin H. Hill, Jr., *Senator Benjamin H. Hill of Georgia, His Life, Speeches, and Writings* (Atlanta: T. H. P. Bloodworth, 1893), 277.

14   Stephen Elliott, *Our Cause in Harmony with the Purposes of God in Christ Jesus. A Sermon Preached in Christ Church, Savannah, on Thursday, September 18, 1862, Being the Day Set Forth by the President of the Confederate States, as a Day of Prayer and Thanksgiving, for our Manifold Victories and Especially for the Fields of Manassas and Richmond, Ky.* By the Rt. Rev. Stephen Elliott, D. D., Rector of Christ Church, and Bishop of the Diocese of Georgia (Savannah: Power Press of John M. Cooper & Co., 1862), 20; Rt. Rev. Stephen Elliott, D. D., *Ezra's Dilemma. A Sermon Preached in Christ Church, Savannah, on Friday, August 21, 1863, Being the Day of Humiliation, Fasting and Prayer, Appointed by the President of the Confederate States.* By the Rt. Rev. Stephen Elliott, D. D., Rector of Christ Church, and Bishop of the Diocese of Georgia (Savannah, GA: Power Press of George N. Nichols, 1863), 12, 13;

Governor Zebulon B. Vance, Inaugural Address, delivered in Raleigh, North Carolina, September 8, 1862, in *Wilmington Journal Weekly*, September 18, 1862; Robert H. Smith, *An Address to the Citizens of Alabama, on the Constitution and Laws of the Confederate States of America, by the Hon. Robert Smith at Temperance Hall, on the 30th of March, 1861* (Mobile: Mobile Daily Register Print, 1861), 19; Watkins, "The South, Her Position and Duty," 5.

15 Stephen Elliot, *"Vain is the Help of Man." A Sermon Preached in Christ Church, Savannah, on Thursday, September 15, 1864, Being the Day of Fasting, Humiliation, and Prayer, Appointed by the Governor of the State of Georgia. By the Rt. Rev. Stephen Elliott, D. D., Rector of Christ Church* (Macon, GA: Burke, Boykin Company, 1864), 11.

16 C. C. Jones, *Religious Instruction of the Negroes. An Address Delivered before the General Assembly of the Presbyterian Church of Augusta, Ga., December* 10, 1861 (Richmond: Presbyterian Committee of Publication, n. d.), 6.

17 *Ibid.*, 6-7.

18 *Ibid.*, 8.

19 Reverend L. Muller, Sermon at Institute Hall, on Fast Day, June 13, 1861, Delivered Before the German Military Companies and German Population, Charleston, South Carolina, in *Charleston Daily Courier*, June 17, 1861.

20 Henry A. Wise, Speech in spring, 1861, date unknown, location unknown [Richmond, June 1, 1861], in *Echoes from the South. Comprising the Most Important Speeches, Proclamations, and Public Acts Emanating from the South during the Late War* (New York: E. B. Treat & Co., 1866), 151; Dr. N. Fisher, Speech Before the Wilkinson Rifle Company, date unknown, in *Milledgeville Federal Union*, May 7, 1861; T. R. R. Cobb, Substance of an Address of T. R. R. Cobb to his Constituents of Clark County, April 6, 1861, n. p., n. d., 5.

21 W. E. Simms, Speech of Hon. W. E. Simms of Kentucky, in reply to Mr. Yancey upon the Amendment to the Exemption bill, proposed by Mr. Dortch, that Justices of the Peace should be liable to Conscription. Delivered in the Senate of the Confederate States, September 15, 1862; in *Richmond Enquirer*, January 10, 1863; Rev. Dr. Palmer, Speech at a barbeque for soldiers of Hampton's Legion, delivered in Columbia, South Carolina, April, 1864, in *Montgomery Daily Advertiser*, May 5, 1864.

22 J. J. D. Renfroe, *"The Battle Is God's." A Sermon Preached Before Wilcox's Brigade, on Fast Day, The 21st August, 1863, Near Orange Court-House, VA. By J. J. D. Renfroe, Chaplain 10th Alabama Regiment.* (Richmond: MacFarlane & Fergusson, 1863), 6; Williamson Oldham, Speech of Hon. W. S. Oldham, of Texas, on the Resolutions of the State of Texas, concerning Peace, Reconstruction and Independence, delivered in the Confederate States Senate, January 30, 1865 (n. p., n. d.), in Center for American History, The University of Texas at Austin, 5.

23 Brigadier-General E. W. Gantt, *Address* (Little Rock: n.p., 1863), in University Archives, Howard-Tilton Memorial Library, Tulane University, New Orleans, Louisiana, 26.

24 [John] Baldwin, Substance of the Remarks of Mr. Baldwin, of Virginia, on Offering "A Bill to Fund the Currency," delivered in Confederate House of Representatives, January 16, 1863, (n. p.), in Special Collections, The Robert W. Woodruff Library, Emory University, Atlanta, Georgia, 3.

25 Elliott, *Our Cause in Harmony with the Purposes of God in Jesus Christ*, 1862, 22–23, 11.

26 Elliott, *Ezra's Dilemma*, 1863, 14.

27 Zebulon B. Vance, Speech on Washington's Birthday, delivered to the citizens of Wilkes County, Hillsborough(?), North Carolina, February 22, 1864, in *Hillsborough Recorder*, March 9, 1864. This shift in attitude was captured effectively in the words of Benjamin Hill. During a Congressional debate in February 1863, he first described slaves in a manner reminiscent of prewar ideology, calling them "the best laborer[s] in the world." However, immediately thereafter came a qualifying statement, a statement that severely ridiculed rather than praised. Slaves, he said, would not work without "compulsion. As well turn a gang of monkeys into your fields as a gang of negroes without a supervisor." Benjamin Hill, remarks in Confederate Senate against a motion to take up the house exemption bill, February 12, 1863, in *Southern Historical Society Papers*, vol. 48 (Richmond: Southern Historical Society, 1941; reprint, Broadfoot Publishing Company, 1992), 105.

28 R. R. Collier, *Remarks on the Subject of the Ownership of Slaves, Delivered by R. R. Collier of Petersburg, in the Senate of Virginia, October 12, 1863* (Richmond: James E. Goode, 1863), 23.

29 Elliott, *Ezra's Dilemma*, 1863, 12.

30 [Thomas] Watts, Synopsis of remarks before the Mass Meeting, held
    in Montgomery, on February 25, 1865, in *Montgomery Daily
    Advertiser*, March 3, 1865. Watts added that before he would accept
    black rule, he would have his "limbs severed from his body and his
    tongue cut out."; Thomas S. Gholson, *Speech of Hon. Thomas S.
    Gholson, of Virginia, on the Policy of Employing Negro Troops, and
    the Duty of all Classes to Aid in the Prosecution of the War.
    Delivered in the House of Representatives of the Congress of the
    Confederate States on the 1st of February, 1865* (Richmond, George P.
    Evans & Co., Printers, 1865), 8.

31 Zebulon B. Vance, Inaugural Address, September 8, 1862.

32 John Parks, *Sermon before Brigadier-General Hoke's Brigade upon
    the Execution of 22 Men for Desertion, 28 February, 1864, At
    Kingston, North Carolina* (Greensboro, NC: A. W. Lincoln & Co.
    Book and Job Printers, 1864), 9. For an example of an antebellum
    planter's use of the term, see Eugene Genovese, *Roll, Jordan, Roll:
    The World the Slaves Made* (New York: Vintage Books, 1976), 649.
    Genovese quotes from an 1857 article on the value of whipping. A
    planter calling himself "Clod Thumper" wrote that "Africans are
    nothing but brutes, and they will love you the better for whipping,
    whether they deserve it or not. . . . To be sure, a half a dozen of
    them may take to the woods, but that is no loss to you." For a
    striking example of deserting soldiers compared to slaves, see
    Wilmington Daily Journal, September 18, 1862, in which a thirty-
    dollar reward was offered for the "apprehension and confinement"
    of Private H. Tredwell, who deserted from camp in August. This
    little notice was printed almost exactly like those for runaway
    slaves, and included much of the same information. Tredwell was
    described as "5 feet 11 inches high, sallow complexion; had on gray
    jacket when he left." In place of the master's name in the lower
    right hand corner, the paper placed the name of Tredwell's captain,
    J. F. Moore.

33 Governor Henry W. Allen, Inaugural Address, 1864, 4.

34 Governor Zebulon B. Vance, Speech on Washington's Birthday,
    February 22, 1864, in *Hillsborough Recorder*, March 9, 1864. Vance
    read part of this statement from a Philadelphia *Inquirer* report.

35 Howell Cobb, Speech at Atlanta, January 28, 1864, in *Rebellion
    Record*, Vol 8 (New York: D. Van Nostrand, 1867), 344.

36 Nathaniel Boyden, Remarks delivered to the Senate of North

Carolina, on the subject of the suspension of the writ of *Habeas Corpus*, date unknown, in *North Carolina Standard*, June 15, 1864.

37 Gholson, 6.

38 H[enry] C. Chambers, Policy of Employing Negro Troops. Speech of Hon. H. C. Chambers, of Mississippi, in the House of Representatives of the Congress of the Confederate States, Thursday, November 10, 1864, on the special order for that day, being the resolution offered by him on the first day of the session . . . (n. p.), 4.

39 Gustavus A. Henry, Speech at the mass meeting at the African Church, Richmond, Virginia, February 9, 1865, in *Richmond Enquirer*, February 13, 1865.

40 J[udah] P. Benjamin, Speech at the mass meeting at the African Church, Richmond, Virginia, February 9, 1865 (paraphrase), in *Richmond Enquirer*, February 10, 1865.

41 Governor Francis Pickens, Speech at Charleston, South Carolina, April 14(?), 1861; Reverend John Parks, Sermon Before Brigadier-General Hoke's Brigade, February 28, 1864, 14.

42 William C. Butler, *Sermon: Preached in St. John's Church, Richmond, Virginia, on the Sunday after the Battle of Manassas, July 21, 1861, by the Rector* (Richmond: Chas. H. Wynne, Printer, 1861), 17.

43 Chas. Minnigerode, *"He that believeth shall not make haste": A Sermon Preached on the First Day of January, 1865, in St. Paul's Church, Richmond* (Richmond: Chas. H. Wynne, Printer, 1865), 9.

44 Henry Foote, Jabez Curry, Remarks in debate on the bill for the burning of cotton, tobacco, and other property, in Confederate House of Representatives, March 5, 1862 (paraphrase), in *Southern Historical Society Papers*, vol. 44 (Richmond: Southern Historical Society, 1923; reprint, Broadfoot Publishing Company, 1991), 101.

45 H. N. Pierce, *Sermons Preached in St. John's Church, Mobile, on the 13th of June, 1861, The National Fast, Appointed by His Excellency Jefferson Davis, President of the Confederate States of America* (Mobile: Farrow & Dennett, Book and Job Printers, 1861), 3, 4; The Reverend J. V. Tucker even went so far as to discuss labor in some detail without once mentioning slaves. In a sermon from 1862, Tucker referred to "our laboring men," and said that "in justice to the laborers and operatives wages should be increased a hundred per cent. . . . the price of labor should go up with everything else."

By laborers, he meant "The clerks in our stores, the mechanics in our shops, and the operative in our factories. . ." Rev. J. V.(?) Tucker, *The Guilt and Punishment of Extortion: A Sermon Preached by Rev. J. V. Tucker, Before his Congregation in Fayetteville, on Sunday, the 7th of September, 1862* (Fayetteville, NC: The Presbyterian Office, 1862), 9, 8.

46   T. R. R. Cobb, Substance of Address to his Constituents, April 6, 1861, (n. p., n. d.), 5.

47   Howell Cobb, Speech at Atlanta, Georgia, May 22, 1861, in *Echoes from the South*, 185.

48   Robert Smith, Address to the Citizens of Alabama, March 30, 1861, 18, 19, 17.

49   Alexander Stephens, "The Corner Stone" Speech in Savannah, Georgia, March 21, 1861, in Cleveland, 721.

50   *Ibid.*, 721.

51   James Henry Hammond, "Mud-Sill" Speech, in Eric L. McKitrick, ed., *Slavery Defended: The Views of the Old South* (Englewood Cliffs, NJ: A Spectrum Book Published by Prentice-Hall, Inc., 1963), 122; Stephens, "The Corner Stone" Speech, 723.

CHAPTER SIX

Gentlemen All:
The Question of Character

In DENYING slaves a meaningful role in the southern war effort, Confederate orators indicated that the responsibility for their nation ultimately rested with whites. The rhetorical analyst, therefore, must next examine the beliefs that white Confederates entertained about themselves and their character. Technically, character is a difficult subject, one far more complex than the discourse on slavery or nature. In addressing the elements of character, including behavior, manners, skills, virtues, and personal accomplishments, orators turned from metaphor to less striking, more indirect forms of communication. Some hinted at acceptable traits through stories and ethical appeals. Some flatly defined appropriate standards of behavior. And, on occasion, some used comparisons or even single words of greeting to convey subtle messages. Consequently, for the study of character, the method of examination must change again. The analyst may no longer rely on a limited number of techniques, but must expand the analysis to include virtually every element of style and technique of argument. The task is both difficult and time-consuming.

However, if carried out properly, analysis reveals that southerners did not assume the burdens of war and nation-building without first determining the personal traits, virtues, and manners they needed for success. And, speeches from the Confederacy's first years show that this creation of a wartime identity involved the disposal of several antebellum traditions.

The process began in early 1861, with assaults on the established convention of rank. Most historians agree that rank was an important factor in the antebellum South, one that ordered behavior and traits of character according to social position. In *Dueling in the Old South,* Jack Williams pointed out how rank controlled behavior on the field of honor, stating "A gentleman fought another gentleman with a pistol. . . . A gentleman horsewhipped or caned a person of the lower estates."[1]

> No gentleman ever accepted a challenge from one not considered his social equal. But who was his social equal? . . . Laboring men and mechanics were not classified as gentry. Businessmen and merchants were suspect, except that bankers were usually highly considered. . . . College teachers were counted as gentlemen . . . planters were gentlemen . . .[2]

Perhaps, though, the best illustration of how rank informed behavior and character comes from Daniel R. Hundley's *Social Relations in Our Southern States.* Writing in 1860, Hundley identified seven distinct groups among whites, each with its own habits, virtues, and traits. Elements of the poorest whites, for example, had "awkward manners, and a natural stupidity or dullness of intellect that almost surpasses belief . . ."[3] Common people, or yeomen, though poor and often illiterate, nonetheless exhibited an "independence of character," great skill with weapons, courage, hospitality, and a strong interest in politics and slavery.[4] The doctors, teachers, farmers, storekeepers, and mechanics of the middle class were industrious, religious, generous, independent, and champions of slavery. And gentlemen manifested physical grace, education, fine manners, and great attraction to politics and the military arts. William Cooper says that Hundley "depicted a society greatly influenced by the power and pretension of social class."[5]

But, when southerners became Confederates, their rhetoric reveals that they immediately sought to dismantle the antebellum concept of rank, turning instead to a more homogenous portrait of their society. "We are brethren," Jefferson Davis told an Alabama crowd in February, 1861, "not in name, merely, but in fact—men of one flesh, one bone, one interest, one purpose. . . . [A]t home we shall have homogeneity."[6] In Georgia, Congressman Daniel Baringer told an April audience that "he can never be a true patriot but always an enemy to his country . . . who endeavors to array the poor against the rich, or the rich against the poor, or any one class of society against another, in a country like ours, . . . we have no 'ranks' in society."[7] And, before the Sunday School Union of Charleston, Congregational minister Thomas Rice used a natural metaphor to emphasize the importance of unity. "When we look into the natural world," he said, "we see an endless variety; but it is always combined with an order and consistency which renders the whole harmonious. Though there is multiplicity, there is unity. The colors of the rainbow are numerous and strongly marked, yet they all unite and blend into one beautiful, grand arch. . . . Let us, in our hearts and efforts, be like these delightful works of God, exhibiting unity in the midst of diversity."[8]

Given the importance of rank in antebellum society, such calls for homogeneity and unity suggest that, in 1861, white southerners

sought a fundamental redefinition of themselves and their character. They wanted, according to one Louisiana speaker, to become
"a new people," bound by a "sacred love of country . . . fighting for
our sovereign rights and bowing in adoration to the August
Majesty on High."[9] Attaining this goal, however, presented some
difficulties. Hundley reveals that no one set of characteristics typ-
ified the southerner, a factor indicating that homogeneity had to
be forged through a selective process. Furthermore, Confederate
discourse shows that Civil War southerners invested character
with a tremendous significance and believed that their chances for
success hinged, in part, on the quality of their citizens. Rice voiced
concern that without "virtue and intelligence in the mass" the
Confederacy might crumble.[10] Similarly, Jefferson Davis linked
victory to the South's ability to show that "we are not degenerate
sons" and that "Southern valor still shines as brightly as in the
days of '76 . . ."[11]

Not surprisingly, therefore, as southerners became
Confederates, they chose to portray themselves as universally gallant and majestic. South Carolinians, according to their Governor
were a "brave people . . . high-toned and chivalrous," and their soldiers beautiful, the "flower, and the hope and the pride" of the
state.[12] Other speakers celebrated Confederate strength, intelligence, and morality, and cheered "the noble-hearted, high-souled,
chivalric women."[13] "The best sentiments of our nature," said a
soldier at a Fourth of July flag ceremony, included "a noble, lofty,
manly patriotism, happily commingled with a gallant and com-
mendable chivalry."[14]

Much of the early Confederate discourse contained similar
words of praise, as both secular and religious speakers joined in
extolling the southern character. If one were to engage such bombast in a purely rhetorical analysis, it might be dismissed simply
as a function of discourse. In *Classical Rhetoric for the Modern*

Student, Edward J. Corbett writes that orators universally associate the virtues of courage, temperance, justice, generosity, prudence, and loyalty with those they seek to compliment. These "common virtues," he states, "figure in discourses of praise."[15] However, when one places the rhetoric about character in its historical context, it becomes but one part of a larger purpose. Southerners, it seems, had a specific persona in mind for their wartime identity, one highly respected before the war. Their boasting and self-promotion were parts of an effort to unite the population under the qualities and attributes of the ideal gentleman.

In the antebellum South, the gentleman was subject to strict codes of ethics and behavior. His status rested partly on his ability to display characteristics regionally associated with "gentility," including grace, wealth, some education, integrity, courtesy, and confidence.[16] Ideally, a gentleman came of "aristocratic parentage" and exhibited "faultless physical development."[17] He was educated in the classics, trained in the military arts, politically active, courteous, and, though generally well-off, uninterested in self-promotion or "mere money-getting."[18] The model gentleman also felt strongly the concept of duty and the need to maintain a "natural dignity of manner" through "the utmost self-possession."[19] He was, Hundley noted, proudly independent, "a man every inch, bold, self-reliant, conscientious; knowing his own convictions of duty, and daring to heed them."[20]

Before secession, these qualifications restricted membership in the gentry to a small percentage of the southern population. In Confederate rhetoric, however, there are striking instances in which speakers flatly advocated transforming the South into a land of elites. Thomas R. Cobb, for example, said in April 1861 that southerners had a duty to "develop in our own people that highest type of man, which combines physical endurance with cultivated intellect, provident forethought with enlarged benevolence, wise statesmanship with enlightened Christianity. . . . To that pristine glory, let us aspire."[21] Likewise, in May, Reverend Rice advocated the use of Sunday schools specifically to raise the "poor, neglected child . . . quite above that grade in society to which his birth assigned him. He would have devoted himself to degrading and vicious pursuits, but the Sabbath School awakened an ambition and implanted principles which elevated the range and widened the scope of his pursuits, . . . to what is good and honorable, philanthropic, and benevolent, and at last he is raised to glory, honor, and immortality."[22]

Much of the discourse from 1861 involved the description and dissemination of attributes once associated with gentlemen. And not surprisingly, definition figured prominently, especially when speakers elucidated behavior and virtues. The Reverend Henry Winkler, for example, instructed a Charleston military company to embrace what he defined as "the character of a model soldier," a character highly reminiscent of the model gentleman. Winkler advised the Moultrie guards to practice temperance, "a comprehensive virtue, especially worthy of the regard of the citizen soldier," as well as justice, "heroism," devotion to God, and mercy. "Spare, whenever you can," Winkler stated, "because a sublime and peculiar dignity belongs to human nature."[23] Sam Houston took a similarly definitive approach in May when he demanded that a crowd of Texans assume "all the heroic virtues which characterize a free people. . . . There must be that sacrificing spirit of patriotism which will yield private desires for the public good. There must be that fortitude which will anticipate occasional reverses . . ." Most importantly, though, southerners needed temperance. "The South," Houston said, "chivalric, brave, and impetuous as it is, must also add to these attributes of success through discipline . . ."[24] Many speakers called for southerners to adopt the gentleman's modesty and sacrifice for the war effort.

They spoke of the need for "noble forbearance," "noble generosity," and self-sacrifice.[25]

But definition was not the only technique orators employed for the promulgation for genteel qualities. In fact, some chose to educate through less authoritarian, more subtle means, an indication that audiences understood and assumed certain traits more easily than others. Few speakers, for example, flatly instructed their listeners to exhibit "manly independence," but preferred instead to promote this virtue through little vignettes or narrative stories. In one case, a speaker cited Roger Taney to illustrate the glory of the individual act of courage. "A native Marylander," James Mason said in June, "he remains at home to defend the last refuge of civil liberty against the atrocious aggressions of a remorseless tyranny. I honor him for it; the world will honor him, . . . and there will be inscribed upon his monument the highest tribute ever paid to a man. He has stood bravely in the breach, and interposed the unspotted arm of justice between the rights of the South and the malignant usurpation of power by the North."[26]

Similarly, in several speeches from Summer, 1861, Howell Cobb promoted independent action through a story about personal sacrifice. The character in this case was an old planter "whose trembling limbs have borne him to his three score and ten years." The elderly gentleman, Cobb said, illustrated the "feelings of our people . . ."

> He was asked, what will you give to sustain our Government in this war?– "Tell them," said he, with the fires of patriotism glowing over all his features, "when my cotton reaches the market, to give me enough for my expenses, and take all the rest." Noble old patriot! And there are thousands and tens of thousands like him all over the South![27]

Through 1861, orators gradually provided audiences with the information needed for refinement and elevation. Those who did not know the proper behavior were taught through definition and illustration. Those who lacked proper, "aristocratic" parentage heard themselves described as the sons of Revolutionary War figures. And those who did not have the proper educational background were offered a fair amount of training by both secular and religious orators. Speakers explained contemporary developments and issues, including the reasons for secession, the Confederate government, and the fiscal details of war bonds, in great detail. They also peppered their discourse with references to the past, thus providing listeners with something of the classical education associated with gentlemen. Indeed, in 1861 alone, listeners were exposed to treatments of the ancient Greeks, the Roman Empire, the American Revolution, Napoleon, the French Revolution, and to quotes from a variety of historical figures. In some cases, orators treated these subjects in great detail. General James Simons, as part of an address at a flag ceremony, chose to provide a brief lecture on the "history and origin of the Zouaves," a subject he discussed for several paragraphs. "The Zouaves," he said,

> were independent tribes of the Province of Constantine in Algeria, who were in the custom of selling their military services to barbarian powers in Africa. The French, between the years 1830 to 1839, sought to make use of these Zouaves as part of the French army in Algeria, and by adding French soldiers to their ranks, and putting the corps under the command of French officers, they hoped to win over the Arabs from their love of country. This effort was attended with little success. The Zouaves deserted in great numbers, and the French could not rely on them, so that by the year 1839, the Zouave Corps ... were composed entirely of Frenchmen. The uniform consisted of turbans, short close waistcoats, and loose flowing trowsers [sic], reaching to the knee, with gaiters below.[28]

Speakers' efforts to mold Confederates into model gentlemen indicate that southerners initially believed that they could assume such an elevated character. However, this activity also suggests that they made the same mistakes in regard to themselves that were made in their depictions of the natural environment. In casting natural beauty as a defining feature of their country, Confederates failed to prepare themselves for the reality of war and its potential for destruction. Similarly, in linking success with their ability to sustain the qualities and traits of the model gentlemen, they established unreasonable expectations for themselves during a particularly trying and arduous period. Even at the best of times, sustaining the moderation, the confidence, the calm detachment, and the humility required of the gentleman was difficult, and a number of antebellum southerners committed indiscretions. Thomas King, a successful sea-island planter from Georgia, craved attention, loved the celebrity status that came with a political career and drank more than his wife preferred. Others, including James Henry Hammond, could not always control their passions and were prone to episodes of sexual misbehavior and outbursts of temper. As Bertram Wyatt-Brown notes, "Gentility . . . involved mastery of quite subtle marks of status . . . and other rules not easy to follow with aplomb."[29]

Thus, the first signs of Confederate declension appeared early, for wartime conditions put a tremendous strain on the civilian population. Shortages appeared almost immediately as the Union blockade restricted imports; by August, 1861, for example, supplies of coffee had dwindled to the point that southerners were drinking brewed okra, barley, or corn.[30] Prices rose steadily until, by 1862, salt, fabrics, meats, tin, and copper were beyond the reach of average citizens. These problems, as one Virginia speaker recognized, made for the first test of Confederate character, the first challenge to their ability to unite, sacrifice, and exhibit the economic disinterest of the gentleman. "The time is past," said the Reverend Stephen Elliot in November, 1861, "for levity, for dissipation. . . . We have now entered upon the work which demands all man's self-possession and woman's self-sacrifice . . ."[31]

Many Southerners, however, failed the test. As often happens in war, some citizens, instead of acting in harmony, promoting generosity, and disdaining "mere money getting," aggressively exploited the situation for personal gain.[32] Some hoarded badly needed food and supplies in hopes of controlling the market and reaping tremendous profits. Businesses fed inflation by continuing to release paper money into the saturated economy, and citizens counterfeited the national currency. In addition, some planters and farmers selfishly refused requests to grow more food than cotton, preferring the risk of grain shortages to decreased profits. As for the military, the flow of volunteers began to decrease by early 1862, stemmed in part by setbacks in Tennessee and North Carolina.

By 1862, Confederate citizens had come to recognize that they were not living up to expectations. In February, the *Richmond Examiner* lamented the selfishness of Confederate citizens. Noting that horses needed by the military were tied up in cab service in Richmond, the paper asked if it were too much that the city population "consent to walk a few squares." The *Examiner* demanded that southerners "practice all the self-denial that the crisis demands" and specifically begged the wealthy to contribute to the war effort through "a temporary sacrifice of useless pleasures."[33] By late 1862 and into 1863, however, with abuses continuing unchecked, Confederate governments embarked on what historian Charles Ramsdell calls an "unprecedented extension of political authority" and began legislating behavior.[34] States took control of agricultural activity and ordered farmers to grow food crops. Those who refused were fined or, in some cases, imprisoned. The distilling of whiskey, a practice that made money for the individual but took food from the country, was restricted across the

South. Civil and military officials seized and distributed the catches of speculators, thereby forcing recalcitrant citizens to share their goods and supplies.[35] And, in April, 1862, the national government began conscripting soldiers, eventually forcing thousands of men to sacrifice their freedom and sometimes their lives in the army.

Government thus responded to civilian intransigence forcefully and dramatically. In contrast, the oratorical response was less trenchant and remained so throughout the balance of the war. Some orators continued to speak in the tones of early 1861, promoting genteel attributes, educating, stressing the importance of harmony, and praising their listeners as gallant and noble. Benjamin Hill, for example, stated in December, 1862 that "A wise government, . . . a gallant army, and a liberal, cordial and united people, constitute together the cause of our progress, the assurance of our success, and our title to admiration and renown."[36] That same year, Senator Charles Russell of Virginia, in a speech before students of the Richmond Medical College, added that southerners "never dream of submission and have no fear of subjugation; . . . have resolved to be free, and have the courage to sustain that high resolve." To Russell, such qualities granted Confederates the right, "therefore, to anticipate a glorious future . . ."[37] In 1864, Gustavus Henry described Confederate citizens as "determined to suffer and endure, [feeling] that suffering and enduring but purify our hearts."[38] And early 1865 found Louisiana Congressman John Perkins stating that southerners would agree with the words of one of the Apostles: *"We are troubled on every side yet not dismayed; we are perplexed, but not in despair; persecuted, but not forsaken; cast down, but not destroyed."* [39] Speakers also continued to offer historical information and thorough explanations of political and economic developments.

But the discourse on character also included some noticeable changes, many of which first appeared in the oratory of the second year. In 1861, nearly every orator spoke optimistically about southerners' ability to assume an elevated character. Many sounded like Alexander Stephens who, as part of his "Cornerstone" speech, told his audience that "Our destiny, under Providence, is in our own hands. . . . We have intelligence, and virtue, and patriotism. All that is required is to cultivate and perpetuate these."[40] In 1862, darker words began to appear in the rhetoric as, for the first time, orators addressed their listeners with scorn and sarcasm. Indeed, as southerners demonstrated their inability to sustain the gentlemanly ideal, speakers responded with verbal assaults against the population. Stephens, in fact, in a November, 1862 address, called profiteering activity one of the "evils of war," and those who participated, "extortioners."[41] Another speaker said that while southerners went hungry, the distilling of grain into whiskey amounted to a "mockery of humanity."[42] In one of the most bitter attacks from 1862, Senator James Phelan viciously denounced the "army of officers whose services are useless, and who only consume the scanty substance of the land." Angrily concluding an oration on conscription, he cried:

> . . . I protest against a policy which shelters at home in slothfulness and repose, the pampered pensionaries of official patronage, when all other classes of our population . . . are bearing aloft the banner of the Confederacy, dripping with their patriotic blood . . .[43]

Most significantly, the depiction of the ideal character also began to change. Starting in 1862, orators increasingly spoke against individuality, advocating that southerners forego "manly independence" for unquestioning obedience and unity. Charles Russell demanded this forcefully in his speech before the Richmond Medical College. "But I invoke you to sustain your government firmly," he ordered the students, "however vigorous, or stern, or severe, its measures may be for a time. Stand by it though it should demand the services of every citizen, . . . and though it may exert the largest powers for the suppression of treason."[44] Likewise, Georgia Senator George Gordon stated that "all of us must make sacrifices in this war." In Gordon's case, that meant "yield[ing] obedience for a time" to a government measure he found unacceptable and relinquishing his right to mount a vigorous opposition.[45] Southerners, according to Governor Vance, needed to accept "a new order of things . . . while the contest lasts, at least, let us see nothing, hear nothing, know nothing but our country and its sufferings."[46]

Unthinking obedience was not a trait of the gentleman, and the celebration of this quality, combined with the scorn some orators were starting to direct at southern citizens, indicates that Confederates were beginning to seek a new behavioral model. In his inaugural address on September 8, 1862, Vance indicated where the new model might be found. Having been elected governor while serving in Virginia, he mounted the podium with battle still fresh on his mind. In his speech, Vance frequently referred to soldiers and, interestingly, began to cite their actions as examples of proper behavior. Arguing for citizens to unite behind conscription, he pointed out that this act "fell hardest upon the patriotic soldiers in the field," men who desperately wanted to return home after already having served for a year. The soldiers, Vance said, might have rebelled or deserted, and their refusal to do so made them the most exemplary beings in the Confederacy. "An exhibition of purer patriotism," he cried, "has not been seen on the continent, and our government can never sufficiently appreciate it." From here, Vance related a story in which soldiers were the principal actors, a dramatic tale about his own regiment's gallant decision to stay in the army and continue to sacrifice.[47]

The rhetorical changes of 1862 heralded an emerging trend in

Confederate oratory, a trend that intensified as conditions within the southern nation deteriorated. One historian calls the middle years of 1863 and 1864 the "weary days" of the Confederacy, when deepening shortages and military reversals caused a noticeable corruption of the southern character.[48] In these years, some citizens abandoned all pretense of concern for their country and totally committed themselves to self-service. Sometimes their behavior was shocking, such as when Union forces took complete control of the Mississippi River in 1863. Many area planters quickly shifted their allegiance back to the United States and profited from selling cotton to the conquerors. Men evaded the draft or deserted the army for careers as highwaymen. State governors selfishly hoarded military supplies, refusing to share blankets and uniforms though soldiers went barefoot and cold. In Richmond, women rioted in the streets in 1863, demanding food and taking bread by force. Furthermore, in 1863 and 1864, Confederates began to question whether they wanted to continue fighting. In South Carolina, once the seat of zealous Confederate nationalism, 1864 found leading newspaper editors and Congressmen calling for a peace convention with the North and for the resignation of President Jefferson Davis.

Confronted with such a collapse of character, orators responded according to the rhetorical framework developed in 1862. They drew sharp distinctions between the civilian and military elements of their society and wholeheartedly endorsed the soldier as the model being. Civilians, on the other hand, were generally treated harshly, subject to denunciations and insults that, prior to 1861, might have provoked challenges.

Before the war, southerners were sensitive to spoken insults and sometimes fought duels over minor offenses. Men issued challenges after being called puppies, shot each other in defense of wives and family, and even let absurd statements drive them to violence. On one occasion, two men took to the field after one called the other an "ugly, gawky, Yankee looking fellow."[49] Some of this sensitivity, however, seems to have faded during the war. Speaking in January, 1863, Mr. Baldwin of Virginia flatly stated that southerners initially "deceived themselves" and their country into thinking they could sustain the war effort, voluntarily, and were subsequently becoming nothing more than "a nation of speculators and extortioners."[50] From Arkansas, General Gantt sneered nastily at Jefferson Davis, claiming that "This gentleman has proven himself totally unsuited. . . ." Gantt depicted the Confederate President as "weak, mean, . . . cold, selfish, and supremely ambitious."[51] In a March, 1863, graduation address, an orator spoke sharply to his audience, warning them that the "selfish will" was "the root of moral evil." If the people did not begin to exhibit "justice, virtue and humanity," he warned, "they may become the prey of the most abject degradation and the most vulgar tyranny."[52]

Towards 1864, Confederate speakers heaped increasing amounts of abuse on their listeners. In November, 1863, a North Carolinian warned that "If we are subjugated it is because of the parsimony of the people," a preliminary comment to the more serious attacks of 1864.[53] Audiences subsequently heard themselves likened to cowards, croakers, and to a mutinous crew whose "habit of assailing the President" rendered "aid and comfort to the enemy." "Are you here cowards," asked a Major Ennett in September, "asking other men to shed their blood for a country that you would not defend with your own? Are you here half-traitors?"[54] Henry Watkins Allen, addressing citizen fears over the strength of the Confederate army, asked "Who is desponding? Let the croaker go to his wife, if he has one, and tie himself to her apron strings, and nurse the children the rest of his days!"[55] Not to be outdone, in April, 1864, Virginia Reverend D. S. Doggett described the wartime South as a "hot-bed of vice." "Rare examples of religion and virtue," he said, "as well as of patriotism, have shed their lustre upon our country, within the last three years." Doggett named such vices as "unblushing profanity, which, like a flood, has overflowed the land," drunkenness, addiction to entertainment, and greed, which, in a moment of grotesque imagery, he said turned citizens into "monsters as moral sharks, vultures, and vampires" that "gorged themselves" with the blood of the nation.[56]

"Ill-omened creatures!" he cried. "They haunt our thoroughfares; they scent the carrion from afar, and collect to make a carnival upon the ebbing life of a nation. . . . What care they if their fangs tear open even the corpse, and their appetite be glutted with the marrow of their murdered victim?"[57] Audiences apparently agreed with these assessments, for speakers were not attacked upon their delivery. Indeed, on one occasion in 1865, an audience member voiced disagreement only when the speaker tried to praise the Confederacy. "We hold more territory now, than we did twelve months ago," said Governor Watts during an Alabama rally. A listener promptly challenged him, stating "Oh, no," whereupon Watts unleashed several insults. He called the heckler a "croaker" and asked, "did I hear some tory deny it?"[58]

By 1864, only soldiers were immune from denunciation and condemnation, having been carefully set apart as the new guardians of southern character. In the same 1863 speech in which a North Carolinian warned his audience that their "parsimony" would lead to subjugation, the speaker also noted that "the soldiers give their health, strength and lives to the country. . . ."[59] Soldiers were described as brave, skilled, patriotic, and obedient. "Have those soldiers filled their contracts?" asked Major Ennett. "Yes; they have. . . . He has been severely wounded . . . all this he bore with a veteran's fortitude; nothing daunted his manly spirit . . ." [60] They "endured privations and sufferings without complaint, met danger and death without faltering, and snatched victory from the jaws of defeat without invidious triumph. They have been patient in suffering, defiant in danger, modest in victory."[60] And when soldiers behaved badly, their actions were sometimes blamed on the civilian population. Speaking after the execution of twenty-two deserters, a North Carolina minister stated, "From all that I have learned in the prison, in the guard house, in the camp, and in the country, *I am fully satisfied, that the great amount of desertions from our army are produced by, and are the fruits of a bad, mischievous, restless, and dissatisfied, not to say disloyal influence that is at work in the country at home.*"[61] [Italics in original.]

Rhetorical analysis thus indicates that southerners improperly prepared themselves for the difficult task of winning a war. In attempting to unify behind the qualities and traits of the gentleman, they established a set of unreasonable expectations from the start. And when they proved incapable of sustaining gentility, southerners seemed to lose something of themselves. From 1862, audiences sat quietly while speakers assailed and denounced them, attempted to shame them into behaving properly, and explained how they were responsible for the downfall of the Confederacy. Civilians were cast as traitors, croakers, tories, and were told, in 1865, that those willing to surrender to the North were cowards. "Great God!" yelled Governor Watts in 1865, "are we the sons of Revolutionary fathers, and have we fallen so low—are we dogs! that we are ready to lick the hand that smites us? Whoever is so base a coward, is unfit to live in a Southern land, is unfit to receive the smiles of Southern women, unfit to be buried in Southern soil!"[62] The only Confederates immune to such attacks were the soldiers.

A number of historians have argued that by 1864 southerners had lost something of their will to fight. The development of southern peace movements, rising disloyalty to the Confederacy and its government, the sorrow expressed in diaries and letters, and the widespread desertions from the army indicate that some type of declension was afoot in Confederate society during the final years of the conflict. Scholars have traced this development to extended political bickering, military reversals, economic woes, shortages, and resentment over government impressment activities. Rhetorical analysis offers an additional explanation. Confederate discourse suggests that southerners, having failed their own expectations of character, turned on themselves. Unable to unite as gentlemen, they instead became traitors, cowards and croakers, titles they accepted without murmur.[63]

Notes

1 Jack K. Williams, *Dueling in the Old South: Vignettes of Social History* (College Station and London: Texas A&M Press, 1980), 26
2 *Ibid.*, 26–28.
3 Daniel R. Hundley, *Social Relations in Our Southern States*, ed. William J. Cooper, Jr. (Baton Rouge and London: Louisiana State University Press, 1979), 264.
4 *Ibid.*, 199.
5 *Ibid.*, xxviii.
6 Jefferson Davis, Speech at Montgomery, Alabama, February 16, 1861, in *Charleston Mercury*, February 18, 1861.
7 Daniel Baringer, Address on the importance of an agricultural education, extract, location unknown, date unknown, in *Milledgeville Federal Union*, April 16, 1861.
8 Reverend Thomas O. Rice, Address before the South Carolina Sunday School Union at their Forty-Second Anniversary, Charleston, South Carolina, May 12, 1861, in *Charleston Daily Courier*, May 16, 1861.
9 Reverend Gierlow, Fast-Day Sermon, extract, date unknown, location unknown, in *Baton Rouge Weekly Gazette & Comet*, December 5, 1861.
10 Rice, Address on May 12, 1861, in *Charleston Daily Courier*, May 16, 1861.
11 Davis, Speech at Montgomery, February 16, 1861, in *Charleston Mercury*, February 18, 1861 The tendency to link success with

character was not unique to the Confederacy, but, rather, an American trait. See Charles Royster, *A Revolutionary People at War: The Continental Army and American Character, 1775–1783* (Chapel Hill: University of North Carolina Press, 1979; reprint, New York and London: W. W. Norton & Company, 1981), 25, 46. Royster states that colonists initially went to war confident that their confidence, virtue, and "'natural' or 'native' or 'innate' courage" ensured victory against British automatons. Generals were at first expected, Royster says, "to perform miracles by force of personality alone." Similar behavior occurred in the Mexican-American War. In this conflict, Americans initially armed themselves with the belief that they were a superior people crusading for liberty against a backward, indolent, and lazy enemy. See James M. McCaffrey, *Army of Manifest Destiny: The American Soldier in the Mexican War, 1846-1848.* The American Social Experience Series, vol. 23, Gen. Ed. James Kirby Martin (New York and London: New York University Press, 1992), 68–69.

12   Governor Francis Pickens, Speech at Charleston, South Carolina, April 14(?), 1861, in *Charleston Daily Courier,* April 15, 1861.

13   A. P. Lining, Speech at Fourth of July celebration, Charleston, South Carolina, July 4, 1861, in *Charleston Daily Courier,* July 6, 1861.

14   Lieutenant Blake, Speech at Fourth of July celebration, Charleston, South Carolina, July 4, 1861, in *Charleston Daily Courier,* July 6, 1861

15   Edward P. J. Corbett, *Classical Rhetoric for the Modern Student,* 3d. ed. (New York: Oxford University Press, 1990), 140.

16   Bertram Wyatt-Brown *Southern Honor: Ethics and Behavior in the Old South* (Oxford and New York: Oxford University Press, 1982).

17   Hundley, 27, 28.

18   *Ibid.,* 58.

19   *Ibid.,* 70–71.

20   *Ibid.,* 63.

21   T[homas] R. R. Cobb, Substance of an Address of T. R. R. Cobb to his Constituents of Clark County, location unknown, April 6, 1861, (n. p., n. d.), 6.

22   Rice, Address on May 12, 1861, in *Charleston Daily Courier,* May 16, 1861.

23   E. T. Winkler, *Duties of the Citizen Soldier. A Sermon Delivered in the First Baptist Church of Charleston, S.C. on Sabbath Morning, January 6, 1861, before the Moultrie Guards, by E. T. Winkler,*

Chaplain of the Company (Charleston: A. J. Burke, 1861), 10, 11, 12, 13, 14, 12.

24 Sam Houston, Speech at Independence, Texas, May 10, 1861, in *Echoes from the South Comprising the most Important Speeches, Proclamations, and Public Acts Emanating from the South during the Late War* (New York: E. B. Treat & Co., 1866), 180.

25 Governor Francis Pickens, Speech at Charleston, South Carolina, April 14(?), 1861, in *Charleston Daily Courier*, April 15, 1861.

26 J[ames] Mason, Speech at Richmond,Virginia, June 8, 1861, in *Echoes From the South*, 168.

27 Howell Cobb, Speech at Atlanta, Georgia, May 29(?), 1861, in *Milledgeville Federal Union*, June 4, 1861.

28 General James Simons, Speech at Eighty-Fifth Anniversary of the Battle of Fort Moultrie, Charleston, South Carlina, June 28, 1861, in *Charleston Daily Courier*, June 29, 1861.

29 Wyatt-Brown, 88 Thomas King information from Steven M. Stowe, who notes that King's wife seems to have expressed concerns about his drinking on more than one occasion. *Intimacy and Power in the Old South: Ritual in the Lives of the Planters*, New Studies in American Intellectual and Cultural History (Baltimore and London The Johns Hopkins University Press, 1987), 225, 226, 230. For information on James Henry Hammond, see Drew Gilpin Faust, *James Henry Hammond and the Old South: A Design for Mastery* (Baton Rouge and London: Louisiana State University Press, 1982), 29, 229. Faust describes Hammond's despair as a young man when he found he was unable to control what an acquaintance called Hammond's "lustful appetite." "With charming and flirtatious women," Faust says, "Hammond found resistance almost impossible. . . . In desperation, he decided to renounce romantic involvement altogether" to protect his self-control. As an adult, she adds, he struggled with a "longing for fame," a desire once he sought to master by "rejecting ambition altogether."

30 Charles W. Ramsdell, *Behind the Lines in the Southern Confederacy*, ed. Wendell H. Stephenson (Baton Rouge: Louisiana State University Press, 1944; reprint, New York: Greenwood Press, Publishers, 1969), 19.

31 Stephen Elliot, *How to Renew our National Strength, A Sermon at Christ Church, Savannah, Georgia, November 15, 1861, on the day of*

Humiliation, Fasting, and Prayer (Richmond: Macfarlane & Fergusson, Printers, 1862), 11.

32 Hundley, 58.

33 John M. Daniel, *The Richmond Examiner During the War, or, The Writings of John M. Daniel*, The American Journalist Series (n.p.: Arno Press, Inc., 1970), 39.

34 Ramsdell, 61.

35 *Ibid.*, 36.

36 Benjamin Hill, Speech Delivered before the Georgia Legislature, in Milledgeville, December 11, 1862 In *Benjamin H. Hill, Jr., Senator Benjamin H. Hill of Georgia, His Life, Speeches, and Writings* (Atlanta: T. H. P. Bloodworth, 1893), 257.

37 Charles W. Russell, Graduation Address before the Richmond Medical College, date unknown, in *Richmond Enquirer*, March 28, 1862.

38 Gustavus A. Henry, Speech of Hon. Gustavus A. Henry of Tennessee, on his joint resolution, defining the position of the Confederate States, and declaring the determination of the Congress and the people thereof to prosecute the war till their independence is acknowledged, delivered in the Confederate Senate, November 29, 1864, (n. p.), 9.

39 John Perkins, Remarks of Honorable John Perkins, of Louisiana, on presenting from the Committee on Foreign Affairs, Resolutions in regard to the Negotiations for Peace, delivered in the Confederate House of Representatives, exact date unknown, 1865, (n. p.), 7-8, quoting from Apostle Paul.

40 Alexander Stephens, Speech delivered in Savannah, Georgia, March 21, 1861, Known as "The Corner Stone Speech," reported in the *Savannah Republican*, in Henry Cleveland, *Alexander Stephens in Public and Private With letters and speeches before, during and since the War* (Philadelphia: National Publishing Company, c. 1866), 725–26.

41 Stephens, Synopsis of the Substance of the Address at Crawfordville, Georgia, on November 1, 1862, reported by J. Henley Smith, in Cleveland, 751.

42 Mr. Smith, Remarks of Mr. Smith, of Macon, on the Ordinance to prohibit, for a limited time, the manufacture of Spirituous Liquors, delivered in the North Carolina Convention, date unknown, in *North Carolina Standard*, March 5, 1862.

43 James Phelan, *Speech of Hon. James Phelan, of Mississippi, on the Motion to Conscript "Justices of the Peace," and Involving the Power of Congress to Exact Military Service of a State Officer. Delivered in the Senate of the Confederate States, Sept. 6, 1862* (Richmond: Enquirer Book and Job Press, 1862), 18.

44 Charles W. Russell, Address Before the Richmond Medical College, March 28, 1862.

45 George Gordon, Speech of Hon. George Gordon, of Chatham, on the Constitutionality of the Conscription Laws Passed by the Congress of the Confederate States, Delivered in the Senate of Georgia on Tuesday, 9th December, 1862, (n. p.), 13, 4.

46 Zebulon B. Vance, Inaugural Address, delivered in Raleigh, North Carolina, September 8, 1862, in *Wilmington Journal Weekly*, September 18, 1862.

47 *Ibid.*

48 Ramsdell, 41.

49 Williams, 22.

50 [John] Baldwin, Substance of the Remarks of Mr. Baldwin of Virginia, on Offering "A Bill to Fund the Currency." Delivered in the Confederate House of Representatives, January 16, 1863 (n. p.), in Special Collections, Robert W. Woodruff Library, Emory University, Atlanta, Georgia, 4, 9.

51 Brigadier-General E. W. Gantt, *Address* (Little Rock: n.p., 1863), in University Archives, Howard-Tilton Memorial Library, Tulane University, New Orleans, Louisiana, 15.

52 James Warley Miles, God in History Extract from a discourse delivered before the graduating class of the College of Charleston, Sunday evening, March 29, 1863, in *Hillsborough Recorder*, May 20, 1863.

53 Governor Smith, Speech on the condition of the country, to the citizens of Petersburg, Virginia, November 4, 1863 (partial paraphrase), in *Hillsborough Recorder*, November 11, 1863.

54 Gustavus A. Henry, November 29, 1864, 12; Major W. T. Ennett, Speech at Turkey Creek School House, North Carolina, September 17, 1864, in *Wilmington Journal Weekly*, October 27, 1864.

55 Governor Henry Watkins Allen, Inaugural Address of Governor Henry W. Allen to the Legislature of the State of Louisiana, delivered at Shreveport, January 25, 1864, (n. p.), in Special Collections, Louisiana State University Libraries, Baton Rouge, Louisiana, 3.

56 D. S. Doggett, *The War and Its Close, A Discourse Delivered in Centenary Church, Richmond, Va., Friday, April 8, 1864, on the Occasion of the National Fast* (Richmond: MacFarlane & Fergusson, 1864), 9, 10–11; for grotesque imagery see also J. J. D. Renfroe, "*The Battle is God's.*" *A Sermon Preached before Wilcox's Brigade, on Fast Day, the 21ˢᵗ of August, 1863, Near Orange Court House, Va. By J. J. D. Renfroe, Chaplain, 10ᵗʰ Alabama Regiment* (Richmond: MacFarlane & Ferguson, 1863), 20. Renfroe said that many Confederate citizens "preyed upon the vitals of the country," and "sucked the blood of the land."

57 *Ibid.*

58 Governor [Thomas] Watts, Synopsis of remarks before the Mass Meeting, held in Montgomery, on February 25, 1865, in *Montgomery Daily Advertiser*, March 3, 1865.

59 Smith, Speech on condition of the country, in *Hillsborough Recorder*, November 11, 1863. Separation of military and civilian also occurred in Congress. See *Southern Historical Society Papers*, vol. 48 (Richmond: Southern Historical Society, 1941), 107. Debating military exemptions and class favoritism, Mr. Wigfall of Texas stated in February, 1863, that "This question . . . does not reach the army–it is made outside." See Mr. Wigfall, Remarks of Mr. Wigfall of Texas, on the Exemption Bill, delivered in Confederate Senate, February 12, 1863, *Southern Historical Society Papers*, vol. 48 (Richmond: Southern Historical Society, 1941; reprint Broadfoot Publishing Company, 1992), 107.

60 Major Ennett, September 17, 1864.

61 Mr. Grissom, Remarks on the adoption of the Majority Resolutions in relation to Habeas Corpus, delivered in North Carolina House of Commons, May 25, 1864, in *North Carolina Standard*, June 1, 1864.

62 Reverend John Parks, *Sermon before Brigadier-General Hoke's Brigade upon the Execution of 22 Men for Desertion, 28 February, 1864, at Kingston, North Carolina* (Greensboro, NC: A W. Lincoln & Co. Book and Job Printers, 1864), 8.

63 Governor [Thomas] Watts, Synopsis of remarks before the mass meeting in Montgomery, February 25, 1865, in *Montgomery Daily Advertiser*, March 3, 1865.

64 For an opposite view in regard to the Confederate loss of will see Gary W. Gallagher, *The Confederate War* (Cambridge and London: Harvard University Press, 1997). Gallagher makes an intriguing argument that challenges traditional interpretations.

CHAPTER SEVEN

Towards a Rhetorical Union

SPEECH ANALYSIS indicates that the Civil War had a highly disruptive effect on the South. Through four years of conflict, Confederate rhetoric underwent dramatic changes. By 1865, subjects once said to evince southern superiority, including the natural environment and civilian character, had come under savage condemnation. And black slaves, once praised as sources of strength and wealth, increasingly became objects of scorn and hatred. The findings of rhetorical analysis therefore agree with those Emory Thomas reported in a seminal work published in 1971. In *The Confederacy as a Revolutionary Experience*, Thomas argued that between 1861 and 1865, "in the name of independence . . . Southerners reversed or severely undermined virtually every tenet of the way of life they were supposedly defending." For the Confederacy, he concluded, the Civil War produced nothing less than an internal revolution.[1]

Rhetorical analysis, though, also opens the door to several intriguing speculations about the nature and direction of the Confederate revolution. Indeed, if one accepts this work's earlier premise that spoken words reflect social context, Confederate discourse suggests first that the Civil War toughened southerners. Speech analysis indicates that the bloody conflict produced a shift in southern thought that corresponds to what David Shi recently suggested in *Facing Facts: Realism in American Thought and Culture, 1850–1920.* Studying the origins and aesthetics of late-nineteenth century American realism, Shi argued that the Civil War played a pivotal role in directing American intellectuals and artists away from antebellum romanticism. The violence and gore of combat, so shockingly different from what Americans had pictured of war, "provided the impetus," Shi wrote, "for at least some writers, artists, critics, and members of the reading and viewing public to look at life through clearer lenses."[2]

This shift is strikingly evident in Confederate rhetoric, manifest in the appearance of whirlpools and storms in the natural environment, in the acknowledgments that slaves could be devious and disloyal, and in the claims that citizens had become selfish and irresponsible. Some orators even spoke openly of the changes they saw in their audiences and talked of how southerners had become hardened by the war. The Reverend Dr. Palmer, for example, speaking to soldiers in Columbia, South Carolina in 1864, noted that men once looked upon as "fond and gentle" fathers had become "grim visaged and determined soldier[s]." Gustavus Henry, also in 1864, argued that southerners understood the nature of war clearly and accepted its tendency to destroy and kill. "We have determined," he said "to suffer and endure, and we feel that suffering and endurance but purify our hearts, and enable us to make sacrifices that are worthy of the cause in which we are engaged. The spirit of patriotism is found in its purest state where the scourge of the oppressor has been most keenly felt. It is then unadulterated, and has been refined of its dross, as silver by fire." Benjamin Hill stated that the conflict had removed much that was unnecessary from the southern character. "Trial," he said in 1865, "is to the national character what the sculptor's chisel is to the marble; it cuts away much of its substance but leaves it in shape, comeliness, and value."[3]

But rhetorical analysis also reveals something about the specific trajectory of the Confederate revolution, especially when one examines certain words and phrases expressed during the war. Throughout the conflict, southern orators spoke extensively about a limited number of subjects. They talked in detail about the Southern environment, the war, the southern people, and their enemies. And when one compares the words and expressions Confederates adopted for themselves and their country to those they reserved for the United States, an interesting suggestion about wartime change emerges. During the conflict, speakers progressively applied what were defined as "northern" qualities to themselves and their nation. Confederate rhetoric, therefore, hints that the South's experience with war and nation-building ultimately directed it back to the North.

Historians have disagreed as to the degree of separation that existed between Union and Confederacy. Many recognize that the war forced the South to develop several northern characteristics, including an industrial sector and an enlarged, active government, but disagree as to whether this circumstance actually drew the antagonists together. Some, like Emory Thomas in *The Confederate Nation*, argue that North and South were dissimilar both before and during the war. Writing in 1979, he concluded that Civil War southerners developed a unique Confederate identity, unlike the North but also distinct from the Old South. Thomas noted that the southern nation evolved some northern characteristics, but asserted that it was hardly a copy of the Union. After all, he argued, the Confederacy developed a unique type of war industry as well as its own history."[4] Other historians, however, question whether the Civil War South achieved even this level of distinctiveness. The writers of *Why the South Lost the Civil War* argue that in the short period from 1861–1865, "It would be unreasonable to expect Confederates to have developed sufficient distinctiveness from their northern brothers to evolve into a separate nationality." As evidence of the close ties between Union and Confederacy, they point out that the southern nation retained United States laws, adopted a near copy of the United States Constitution, and celebrated United States Presidents, including Andrew Jackson and Thomas Jefferson, on postage stamps.[5]

The findings of speech analysis fall directly into the center of this debate. When the words spoken about the North are taken under examination, they indicate that southerners initially sought to distance themselves from their enemy, but never articulated a decisive separation. At times, orators spoke directly to the differences between North and South, contrasting southern chivalry with northern brutality, treachery, tyranny, and greed. James Mason, for example, noted how avarice separated the opposing sides, stating "They [northerners] are mercenaries fighting for pay, you are men fighting for your homes and rights." Alexander Stephens postulated that North and South differed in their abilities to appreciate freedom. "They never understood it," he said in June, 1861; "Constitutional liberty is a plant of Southern growth, watered by Southern hands, nurtured by Southern hands. ... At the North there is anarchy." And, after accusing northerners of terrible crimes, a Virginia Congressman concluded "we make mild-mannered war on armies only and they make savage war on defenseless citizens . . ."[6] Under condemnation, northerners were said to support rape, murder, and kidnapping, to trample the

Constitution, and to ignore the word of God. Many a speaker further decreed that northern savagery caused irreparable damage to
the future relationship between United and Confederate States. In
January, 1865, Williamson Oldham questioned whether southerners could ever forget northern crimes "against humanity, against
God" or whether they could, "by any means, be induced to live in
reunion with the perpetrators. . . ?"[7]

This bitter invective stands out clearly and can mislead the analyst into believing that southerners separated themselves from
their enemies behind a wall of hatred. Speakers, however, also
acknowledged northern intelligence, bravery, power, and financial might. They talked of the discipline, ingenuity, and prosperity
of the northern people and spoke sorrowfully of how the war pit-
ted brother against brother.[8] The Reverend Gierlow of Louisiana
even asked that southerners foster a degree of compassion for
their enemies. In August 1861, during a sermon in Baton Rouge,
Gierlow requested that his audience "defend our rights . . . with as
little malice and hatred as the punishment of a malefactor by the
judge." "Consider who our enemies are," he said. "Are they not the
workmanship of God's hands?"[9] As the war progressed, speakers
noted their foe's "vast armies," the "intelligent northern mind,"
and the North's ability to absorb the costs of war. "Recall," said one
minister, "the vast, the inexhaustible resources of our enemy in
the men and the materials of war, compared with our own . . ."[10]

The mixture of praise and condemnation Confederates
bestowed on the North indicates that from the start of the war they
felt a paradoxical array of emotions towards their enemies. After
1863, though, speakers began talking increasingly of the ties
between the Confederacy and the United States. In Texas, Sam
Houston joined Union and Confederacy through a discussion of
war weariness. Speaking of the desolation and lack of unity in the
South, Houston noted that northerners also tired of the war and

had their own problems with "discord and discontent." "The people of the Northwest," in particular, he predicted, would not "be so base and despicable as to submit to the . . . usurpations which they have condemned at the ballot box." [11] Reverend Burrows noticed with sorrow that the South was becoming like the North in February, 1863. Unhappy that Richmond, Virginia, was opening a new theater, he stated that "We are to have inaugurated, to-morrow night, in this capital of our new Confederacy, one of these nefarious establishments, which have been the disgrace of European and Northern cities, to be conducted on precisely the same principles . . ." [12]

Additional links between South and North were drawn through 1864 and 1865. Gustavus Henry claimed in November, 1864, that Confederates were "equals in all respects with our enemies," while North Carolinian Josiah Turner spoke of the "two colossal powers of the new continent. . . . The North, old, rich, crafty, and more perfidious than Carthage. The South, young, poor, robust, and brave as Rome. . . . Grant, the North man, bold, dashing and enterprising. . . . Lee, God love him, patient[?], enduring and patriotic . . ." [13] Even some of the most ardent Confederate supporters voiced this tendency to connect. In January, 1865, though Kentucky secessionist Humphrey Marshall angrily asserted that "They can never win us back; never! never!" he also pointed out that southerners would benefit from borrowing northern styles of war. First drawing distinctions between North and South, he stated that combat

has been conducted by the United States with an atrocity and disregard of humanity that has no parallel upon the records of any civilization. We have met it thus far with fair blows and in a spirit at least of Christian chivalry.

But, the fact is THIS STATE OF THINGS MUST CHANGE. . . . the blood of the Southern people can be roused to a pitch. WHEN IT

WILL RETALIATE, IN KIND, . . . THERE SHALL BE NO SAFETY ANY-
WHERE [original emphasis].

According to the *Richmond Whig*, Marshall concluded that "he would practice the same kind of warfare they do," and added that "We can throw off civilization as well as our neighbors."[14]

But the most striking evidence that southerners were moving closer to the North appears in their rhetoric from 1864 and 1865. Early in the war, Confederate speakers established a core group of characterizations they used to denounce the North: the region was cold and frozen, its people were ambitious, irreverent towards the Constitution, tyrannical, and lacking faith in and respect for God. These characterizations were applied to the North throughout the war. Rhetorical analysis, however, also reveals that as orators began castigating the South and its people, they often did so by appropriating terms once specifically reserved for the North.

The most obvious example of this behavior may be found in the manner in which orators discussed the environment. At first Confederates repeatedly linked the North with cold and ice. John Gilmer, speaking to the United States House of Representatives even before his state of North Carolina seceded, accused north-erners of expressing a "cold, icy, stoical indifference" towards southern concerns. In February, 1861, while urging Virginia to leave the Union, Henry Benning of Georgia noted that southern "winters are shorter and winter days longer than those of the North." Similarly, in June, a South Carolinian commented on the "frozen seas of the North," while Benjamin Hill in 1862 contrasted the "heats and life-destroying miasmas of the tropical South" with the "frozen snows and icy winds of the chilly North."[15] Several ora-tors vividly described the bitter conditions at Valley Forge, Pennsylvania, during the Revolution, and Albert G. Brown, in 1863, advocated driving northerners "back to the icy regions from which they come."[16]

By 1864, however, icy imagery began to appear increasingly in reference to the South. General Gantt described defeated Confederate soldiers in Arkansas as "shattered columns," marching "over snow and ice," while Joseph Echols in 1865 told of "Our soldiers, who are now enveloped in mud and snow." The Reverend Charles Minnigerode talked of an earlier prediction that some Confederates "would wax cold in the hour of danger," and John Baldwin, speaking defiantly at a Richmond rally, acknowledged that the army was on the verge of wasting "away from starvation and cold."[17]

Speakers also began to apply their perception of the North's lack of religious faith to the Confederacy. In 1861, North and South were cast as diametric opposites on the subject of Christianity and worthiness before God. Many orators specifically called northerners "faithless," while others equated the United States with the "demon," the "serpent . . . in our Eden," the "ungodly government" that "fears not God."[18] The North, according to Alexander Stephens, fought an arrogant "crusade to make things better than the Creator made them, or to make things equal, which he [sic] made unequal."[19]

In contrast, speakers described the South as a humble, pious, Christian nation. Thomas Cobb, who once held up work on the Confederate Constitution to debate whether certain government employees should work on Sunday, said that southerners cultivated "the most pure unadulterated, simple Christian Faith, that the world now contains."[20] Aware of their "utter dependence upon Deity" and filled with "reverence for the word and the worship of God," southerners repeatedly proclaimed that God favored the Confederacy and would offer His protection and defense.[21] "He will fight with us again," a Georgia Colonel stated flatly during an address to Georgia volunteers in Virginia. "He loves valor, and He loves a valiant soldier. He will help us . . ."[22] In Charleston, a chaplain agreed. In battle, said the Reverend E. T. Winkler, "Heaven's glory and blessedness will be imparted," given that Confederate soldiers "resort to that God who reveals himself in the gospel, as the Savior of his penitent and believing people."[23]

But by the end of the war the rhetoric had changed, and southerners were said to have adopted the ungodly behaviors of the North. In March, 1863, a graduation speaker told Charleston College students that "When nations or individuals violate those eternal principles of right which Providence has implanted . . . they must suffer the penalty . . ."[24] And, just as the North had been linked to an evil biblical figure–he serpent–Brown linked southern speculators with the "money changers" of the New Testament and to Judas who "betrayed the Savior, but . . . had the decency to hang himself."[25]

Southerners also became "faithless" in Confederate oratory and thus took on a label once assigned exclusively to the North. "Is it not want of faith," asked a speaker in January 1865, "which is the root of all that murmuring against God's providence, that impatience at delay and the frustration of our plans . . . ?" "In all this," he added, ". . . there is no principle except our fickleness and unbelief; there is no firmness, no greatness, no manliness; certainly there is no faith."[26] A speaker in Alabama sadly concluded, "We have met with some serious reverses, probably owing to the sins of those of us at home . . . not showing sufficient dependence in God." "Are we faithless" asked a Georgia minister in 1863, "the moment that God withdraws himself for a little while. . . ?"[27]

The transposition of language also included words about the abuse of constitutional liberties. Confederate orators initially cast northerners as despotic and, in particular, tyrannical. Northerners, it was said, were so concerned with gaining power and control that they destroyed the Constitution and its guarantees of freedom. "It was their folly, their recklessness and their ambition, not ours," said Mississippian Fulton Anderson in 1861, "which shattered into pieces this great Confederated Government, and destroyed this great temple of constitutional liberty..."[28] Alexander Stephens agreed in July 1861, that "the Confederate States to-day rescued the Constitution. . . . a change of government has taken place at the North. The Constitution of our fathers has already been trampled in the dust." Many speakers cast the North as a predator, as a region that desired nothing more than to conquer and enslave the South in order to subject its people to countless humiliations. Northerners, said one southerner, hated easily, had no tolerance, and hoped to inflict on the South "Despotism–the despotism of military force..."[29]

But by 1864, when the Confederate Congress granted President Jefferson Davis broad authority to suspend habeas corpus and declare martial law, a number of speakers accused the Confederate government of the same abuses they once assigned to the North. Just as the North was said to usurp "powers not delegated in the Constitution, which foreshadowed the establishment of an absolute tyranny over these States," the Confederate government was accused of behaving in a "manifestly unconstitutional" manner and inflicting "an outrage upon the public justice of the country."[30] "How came the footsteps of Congressman so suddenly diverted," asked one speaker, "from the pathway of freedom to the goal of tyranny? How came the Goddess of liberty ... to lie down, in the very midset of her devotees, in the lecherous embrace of the cloven-footed satyr of despotism?"[31] Nathaniel Boyden of North Carolina further warned that southerners needed to "maintain and support" their Constitution "against all assaults, no matter from what source they come, and we are as much bound to maintain it against the assaults of Congress..."[32]

In conclusion, rhetorical analysis reveals an interesting line of speculation. It suggests that Southerners began the war unable to thoroughly condemn and separate themselves from the North. As their efforts to achieve independence failed, Confederates reacted by moving closer to their enemy. They drew comparisons, equated themselves with the United States and, by 1864, freely applied what had been defined as northern qualities to their own nation. In Confederate rhetoric, the North started the war condemned as a cold, faithless, tyrannical, ambitious nation. By 1865, the South was described as icy, faithless, and threatened by the tyranny of its own government. Southerners had also become as "ambitious and greedy" as their counterparts in the United States.[33] Just as speakers sneered at the North for its love of money and ambition, its "mercenaries fighting for pay," and its search for "plunder and spoils," by the end of the war, they were condemning southerners for "seeking to make their fortunes at others' expense," and for "worshipping the mighty dollar."[34] The Civil War, in other words, affected a level of rhetorical union between North and South.

Notes

1 Emory M. Thomas, *The Confederacy as a Revolutionary Experience* (Englewood Cliffs, NJ: Prentice-Hall, Inc., c 1971), 134.

2 David E. Shi, *Facing Facts: Realism in American Thought and Culture*, 1850-1920 (New York and Oxford: Oxford University Press, 1995), 65.

3 Reverend Dr. Palmer, Speech at a barbeque for soldiers of Hampton's Legion, delivered in Columbia, South Carolina, April, 1864, in *Montgomery Daily Advertiser*, May 5, 1864; Gustavus Henry, Speech of Hon. Gustavus A. Henry, of Tennessee, on his joint resolution, defining the position of the Confederate States, and declaring the determination of the Congress and the people thereof to prosecute the war till their independence is acknowledged, delivered in the Confederate Senate, November 29, 1864, n. p., n. d., 9; Benjamin H. Hill, Speech Delivered at La Grange, GA., March 11, 1865, in Benjamin H. Hill, Jr., *Senator*

Benjamin H. Hill of Georgia; His Life, Speeches, and Writings
(Atlanta: T. H. P. Bloodworth, 1893), 274.

4 Emory M. Thomas, *The Confederate Nation: 1861–1865*, The New
American Nation Series, eds. Henry Steele Commager and Richard
B. Morris (New York: Harper & Row, Publishers, 1979), 222, 212.
Thomas says that Confederate war industries were developed in a
distinctly southern manner. The South's industrialists, for example,
did not resemble their northern counterparts, for many were
teachers or military men, rather than managers or mechanics.

5 Richard E. Beringer, Herman Hathaway, Archer Jones, William N.
Still, Jr., *Why the South Lost the Civil War* (Athens and London:
University of Georgia Press, 1986), 75, 76–77.

6 J[ames] M[urray] Mason, Speech at Richmond, Virginia, June 8,
1861, in *Echoes from the South, Comprising the most Important
Speeches, Proclamations, and Public Acts Emanating from the South
during the Late War* (New York: E. B. Treat & Co., 1866), 171;
Alexander Stephens, Speech at Augusta, Georgia, delivered July 11,
1861, in Frank Moore, ed., *The Rebellion Record: A Diary of
American Events with Documents, Narratives, Illustrative Incidents,
Poetry, etc.*, vol. 2 (New York: D. Van Nostrand, 1866), 282; Charles
W. Russell, Speech of Hon. Charles Russell of Virginia, on
Retaliation, delivered in Confederate House of Representatives,
October 1, 1862, in *Richmond Enquirer*, October 10, 1862.

7 Williamson Oldham, Speech of Hon. W. S. Oldham, of Texas, on the
Resolutions of the State of Texas, Concerning Peace,
Reconstruction, and Independence, delivered in Confederate
Senate, January 30, 1865, (n. p.), in Center for the Study of American
History, The University of Texas at Austin, Austin, Texas, 12.

8 For examples of praise for the North, see Reverend H. N. Pierce,
*Sermons Preached in St. John's Church, Mobile, Alabama, on the 13th
of June, 1861, The National Fast, Appointed by His Excellency
Jefferson Davis, President of the Confederate States of America*
(Mobile: Farrow & Bennett, Book and Job Printers, 1861), 5. Pierce
said "Our foe is more wily, powerful and brave than the men of this
generation and this land have previously been called upon to meet.
. . . It is ever dangerous to despise an enemy." See also Sam
Houston, Speech at Independence, Texas, May 10, 1861, in *Echoes
From the South*, 180. Houston claimed that "The Northern people
. . . are capable of great endurance and a high state of discipline.

A good motto for a soldier is, Never underestimate the strength of your enemy."

9   Reverend J. Gierlow, A View of the Present Crisis. Sermon by Rev J. Gierlow, Rector of St. James Church, Baton Rouge, Louisiana, August, 1861, (n. p.), 6. Source unknown.

10 Governor Zebulon B. Vance, Inaugural Address, delivered in Raleigh, North Carolina, September 8, 1862, in *Wilmington Journal Weekly*, September 18, 1862; Henry C. Chambers, Policy of Employing Negro Troops, Speech of Hon. H[enry] C. Chambers, of Mississippi, in the House of Representatives of the Congress of the Confederate States, Thursday, November 10, 1864, on the special order for that day, being the resolution offered by him on the first day of the session . . . (n. p.), 4; Reverend D. S. Doggett, *A Nation's Ebenezer. A Discourse Delivered in the Broad St. Methodist Church, Richmond, Virginia, Thursday, September 18, 1862: The Day of Public Thanksgiving, Appointed by the President of the Confederate States* (Richmond: Enquirer Book and Job Press, 1862), 12.

11 Sam Houston, Speech at Houston, Texas, March 18, 1863, in *Memphis Daily Appeal*, April 16, 1863.

12 Pastor J. L. Burrows, *The New Richmond Theater. A Discourse, Delivered on Sunday, February 8, 1863, in the First Baptist Church, Richmond, VA* (Richmond: Smith, Bailey, & Co., 1862), 12.

13 Gustavus A. Henry, Speech of Hon. Gustavus A. Henry, of Tennessee, on his joint resolution, defining the position of the Confederate States, and declaring the determination of the Congress and the people thereof to prosecute the war till their independence is acknowledged, delivered in the Confederate Senate, November 29, 1864 (n. p.), 3; Josiah Turner, Remarks of Hon. Josiah Turner, of North Carolina, on the Resolutions Proposing Negotiations for Peace with the Enemy, delivered in Confederate Congress, date unknown, in *Hillsborough Recorder*, January 4, 1865; Hon. H[umphrey] Marshall, Sketch of the Remarks of Hon. H. Marshall, of Kentucky, made in the House of Representatives of the Confederate States Congress, 15th January, 1865, in *Richmond Whig*, January 23, 1865.

14 Josiah Turner, Remarks of Hon. Josiah Turner, of North Carolina, on the Resolutions Proposing Negotiations for Peace with the Enemy, delivered in Confederate Congress, date unknown, in *Hillsborough Recorder*, January 4, 1865; Hon. H[umphrey] Marshall,

Sketch of the Remarks of Hon. H. Marshall, of Kentucky, made in
the House of Representatives of the Confederate States Congress,
15th January 1865, in *Richmond Whig*, January 23, 1865.

15 John A. Gilmer, Speech in the United States House of
Representatives, January 26, 1861, in *Hillsborough Recorder*,
February 13, 1861; Henry L. Benning, Speech before the Virginia
State Convention, February 14, 1861, in *Rebellion Record*,
supplement to vol. 1 (New York: D. Van Nostrand, 1866), 152;
Reverend L. Muller, Sermon at Institute Hall, on Fast Day, June 13,
1861, Delivered Before the German Military Companies and
German Population, Charleston, South Carolina, in *Charleston
Daily Courier*, June 17, 1861; Benjamin Hill, Speech Delivered before
the Georgia Legislature, in Milledgeville, December 11, 1862, in
Benjamin H. Hill, Jr., *Senator Benjamin H. Hill of Georgia; His Life,
Speeches, and Writings* (Atlanta: T. H. P. Bloodworth, 1893), 271.

16 For a description of Valley Forge see Reverend A. M. Randolph,
*Address on the Day of Fasting and Prayer Appointed by the President
of the Confederate States, June 13, 1861, Delivered in St. George's
Church, Fredericksburg, Virginia* (Fredericksburg: Recorder Job
Office, 1861), 10. Randolph cited "that memorable winter when the
little army of Washington crouched naked and starving upon the
bleak snows of Valley Forge. . . . they heard only the winter's wind
rattling through the bare trees, and gazed upon a cheerless
landscape and a leaden sky . . ." A[lbert] G[allatin]State of the
Country Speech of Hon. A[lbert] G[allatin] Brown of Mississippi,
delivered in the Confederate Senate, December 24, 1863, (n. p.), 1.

17 Brigadier-General E. W. Gantt, *Address*, (Little Rock: n.p., 1863, in
University Archives, Howard-Tilton Memorial Library, Tulane
University, New Orleans, Louisiana, 12; Joseph Echols, Speech in
Confederate House of Representatives, January 19, 1865, in
opposition to a motion to recommit a bill to seize all the cotton
and tobacco of the Confederacy (n. p.), 3; Reverend Chas.
Minnigerode, *"He that believeth shall not make haste." A Sermon
Preached on the First of January, 1865, in St. Paul's Church,
Richmond, By the Rector* (Richmond: Chas. H. Wynne, Printer,
1865), 6; Colonel John Baldwin, Speech delivered at the Capitol,
Richmond, Virginia, February 9, 1865 (paraphrase), in *Richmond
Enquirer*, February 13, 1865.

18 Samuel Hall, Remarks of the Commissioner from Georgia before
the General Assembly of North Carolina, February 13, 1861, in

Wilmington Journal Weekly, February 14, 1861; Master Silas Bunch, Address Delivered at the Anniversary of the Charleston Orphan House, Charleston, South Carolina, October 18, 1861, in *Charleston Mercury,* November 15, 1861; Reverend A. M. Randolph, *Address on the Day of Fasting and Prayer,* June 13, 1861, 7; Reverend W. H. Watkins, The South, Her Position and Duty. A Discourse Delivered at the Methodist Church, Natchez, Mississippi, January 4, 1861, (n. p.), in Mississippi Department of Archives and History, Jackson, Mississippi, 6.

19 Stephens, Speech at Augusta, Georgia, July 11, 1861, 281.

20 T[homas] R. R. Cobb, Substance of an Address of T. R. R. Cobb to his Constituents of Clark County, April 6, 1861 (n.p., n. d.), 6.

21 Bunch, Address at Charleston, October 18, 1861; E. T. Winkler, *Duties of the Citizen Soldier. A Sermon Delivered in the First Baptist Church of Charleston, S. C., on Sabbath Morning, January 6, 1861, before the Moultrie Guards. By E. T. Winkler, D. D., Chaplain of the Company* (Charleston: A. J. Burke, 1861), 13.

22 Colonel Thomas, Speech at camp near Centreville, Virginia, October 17, 1861, in *Wilmington Daily Journal,* November 7, 1861.

23 Winkler, Sermon before Moultrie Guards, January 6, 1861, 10.

24 James Warley Miles, God in History Extract from a discourse delivered before the Graduating Class of the College of Charleston, Sunday evening, March 29, 1863, in *Hillsborough Recorder,* May 20, 1863.

25 A[lbert] G[allatin] Brown, State of the Country Speech, December 24, 1863, 14.

26 Reverend Charles Minnigerode, Sermon of January 1, 1865, 4, 5. In this sermon, Minnigerode also referred to "our own coward, faithless, selfish hearts," 7.

27 Governor [Thomas] Watts, Synopsis of remarks before the Mass Meeting, held in Montgomery, on February 25, 1865, in *Montgomery Daily Advertiser,* March 3, 1865; Rt. Reverend Stephen Elliott, *Ezra's Dilemma. A Sermon Preached in Christ Church, Savannah, On Friday, August 21st, 1863, Being the Day of Humiliation, Fasting and Prayer, Appointed by the President of the Confederate States, by the Rt. Rev. Stephen Elliott, D. D., Rector of Christ Church, and the Bishop of the Diocese of Georgia* (Savannah, GA: Power Press of George N. Nichols, 1863), 16.

28 Fulton Anderson, Speech before the Virginia State Convention, February 14, 1861, in *Rebellion Record,* supplement to vol 1, 144.

29 Stephens, Speech on July 11, 1861, 281; Hon A. W. Terrell, *Oration Delivered on the Fourth Day of July, 1861, at the Capitol, Austin, Texas* (Austin: John Marshall & Co., 1861), 16.

30 Gustavus A. Henry, Speech on his joint resolution, November 27, 1864, 4; Nathaniel Boyden, Remarks delivered to the Senate of North Carolina, on the subject of the suspension of the Writ of *Habeas Corpus*, date unknown, in *North Carolina Standard*, June 15, 1864.

31 Mr. Grissom, Remarks upon the adoption of the Majority Resolutions in relation to *Habeas Corpus*, delivered in North Carolina House of Commons, May 25, 1864, in *North Carolina Standard*, June 1, 1864. See also Hon. John P. Murray, Speech of Hon. John P. Murray, of Tennessee, in favor of repealing the act suspending the privilege of the writ of *habeas corpus*, 1864? (n. p.), 8. Murray called the suspension the work of "military despots."

32 Boyden, Remarks in North Carolina Senate, June 15, 1864.

33 Muller, Sermon at Charleston, June 13, 1861.

34 Mason, Speech at Richmond, June 8, 1861, 171; Joseph Echols, Speech on January 19, 1865, 3; Major Ennett, Speech at Turkey Creek School House, North Carolina, September 17, 1864, in *Wilmington Journal Weekly*, October 27, 1864.

BIBLIOGRAPHY

MANUSCRIPT COLLECTIONS

Coghill, Jonathan Fuller Confederate Letters. 1862–1864. Archives and Manuscripts Department, Auburn University Library, Auburn, Alabama.

Crowder Family Papers. 1861–1862. Archives and Manuscripts Department, Auburn University Library, Auburn, Alabama.

Dehay, Elizabeth Papers. 1862, 1864. Mississippi Department of Archives and History. Jackson, Mississippi.

Dent, Hubert. Letters in Dent Confederate Collection. 1860–1865. Archives and Manuscripts Department, Auburn University Library, Auburn, Alabama.

George, Charles H. Letters in George Confederate Letters. 1863–1864. Archives and Manuscripts Department, Auburn University Library, Auburn, Alabama.

Moore, Robert, Diary. 1861–1863. Mississippi Department of Archives and History. Jackson, Mississippi.

Oldham, William Simpson. "Last Days of the Confederacy," 1869 Typed Manuscript. Center for American History, The University of Texas at Austin.

Overton, Walter Alexander, Diary. 1860–1862. Mississippi Department of Archives and History. Jackson, Mississippi.

Pack, Joseph B. Papers. 1861–1862. South Caroliniana Library Archives. Columbia, South Carolina.

Patrick, John, Diary. 1861–1865. South Caroliniana Library Archives. Columbia, South Carolina.

Ross Civil War Letters, Confederate Collection. 1863. Archives and Manuscripts Department, Auburn University Library, Auburn, Alabama.

Speake-McCalla Civil War Correspondence. 1863–1865. Archives and Manuscripts Department, Auburn University Library, Auburn, Alabama.

York, Emily Smith Papers. 1863–1864. Archives and Manuscripts Department, Auburn University Library, Auburn, Alabama.

NEWSPAPERS

Arkansas State Gazette (Little Rock, Arkansas). 1861.

Bellville Countryman (Bellville,Texas). 1863–1865. Center for American History, The University of Texas at Austin.

Charleston Courier (South Carolina). 1861–1865.

Charleston Mercury (South Carolina). 1861–1865.

Daily Constitution (Augusta, Georgia). 1861.

Dallas Herald (Texas). 1863. Center for American History, The University of Texas at Austin.

Georgia Telegraph (Macon, Georgia). 1861–1863.

Hillsborough Recorder (North Carolina). 1861–1865.

Memphis Daily Appeal (Tennessee). 1861–1865.

Milledgeville Federal Union (Georgia). 1861–1865.

Montgomery Advertiser (Alabama). 1861–1865.

North Carolina Standard (Raleigh, North Carolina). 1862–1865.

Richmond Daily Examiner (Virginia). 1861–1865.

Richmond Enquirer (Virginia). 1861–1865.

Richmond Whig (Virginia). 1865.

Shreveport Semi-Weekly News (Louisiana). 1862–1863.

Southern Confederacy (Atlanta, Georgia). 1862.

Tri-Weekly State Gazette (Austin, Texas). 1863. Center for American History, The University of Texas at Austin.

West Baton Rouge Sugar Planter (Louisiana). 1861.

Wilmington Daily Journal (North Carolina).

Wilmington Journal Weekly (North Carolina).

Vicksburg Daily Whig (Mississippi). 1862–1863.

SPEECHES

Unless otherwise noted, all unpublished speeches from *Confederate Imprints, 1861–1865: Based on Crandall, Marjorie Lyle, Confederate Imprints, 1955, and Harwell, Richard B., More Confederate Imprints, 1957.* Woodbridge, CN: Research Publications, 1974. Microfilm Reels.

Allen, Governor Henry Watkins. Inaugural Address of Governor Henry W. Allen to the Legislature of the State of Louisiana, Delivered at Shreveport, January 25, 1864. n.p., n.d. In Special Collections, Louisiana State University Libraries, Baton Rouge, Louisiana.

Anderson, Fulton, Henry L. Benning, John S. Preston. Speeches before the Virginia State Convention, February 14, 1861. In Frank Moore, ed. *The Rebellion Record: A Diary of American Events with Documents, Narratives, Illustrative Incidents, Poetry, Etc.* Supplement Vol. 1, New York: D. Van Nostrand, 1866.

Baldwin, John (Col.), Colonel Fenston, Hon. John B. Goode. Speeches delivered at the Capitol, Richmond, Virginia. Paraphrase. February 9, 1865. In *Richmond Enquirer*, February 13, 1865.

Baldwin, [John] (Mr.). Substance of the Remarks of Mr. Baldwin, of Virginia, on Offering "A Bill to Fund the Currency." Delivered in Confederate House of Representatives, January 16, 1863. n.p., n.d. Special Collections, The Robert W. Woodruff Library, Emory University, Atlanta, Georgia.

Baringer, Daniel (Hon.). Address on the importance of an agricultural education. Extract, location unknown, date unknown. In *Milledgeville Federal Union*, April 16, 1861.

Beall, Miss Maxa A. Speech Before the Wilkinson Rifle Company, date unknown. In *Milledgeville Federal Union*, May 7, 1861.

Benedict, Reverend Samuel. *The Blessed Dead Waiting for Us, A Sermon Preached in St. James Church, Marietta, Georgia, on the Festival of All Saints, November 1st, 1863.* Macon, GA: Burke, Boykin & Co., Steam Book and Job Printers, 1863.

Benjamin, Judah P. See Robert Mercer Hunter.

Blake, J. A. (Lt.). See A. P. Lining.

Blitch, J. L. (Rev.). *"Thy Kingdom Come." A Sermon Preached to the Aberdeen Church by their Pastor.* Augusta, GA: Baptist Banner Press, 1865.

Boyce, Mr. Speech to his Constituents, delivered in Columbia, November, 1864, in *Hillsborough Recorder*, November 26, 1864.

Boyden, Nathaniel. Remarks delivered to the Senate of North Carolina, on the subject of the suspension of the writ of *Habeas Corpus*, date unknown. In *North Carolina Standard*, June 15, 1864.

Brown, A[lbert] G[allatin]. State of the Country. Speech of Hon. A. G. Brown of Mississippi, delivered in the Confederate Senate, December 24, 1863. n. p., n. d.

Bruce, E. M. (Hon.). Remarks of Hon. E. M. Bruce of Kentucky, in the House of Representatives of the Confederate States of America, June 9 and 10, 1864. n.p., n.d.

Bunch, Master Silas. Address Delivered at the Anniversary of the Charleston Orphan House, Charleston, South Carolina, October 18, 1861. In *Charleston Mercury*, November 15, 1861.

Burrows, Rev. J. L. *Nationality Insured! Notes of A Sermon Delivered at the First Baptist Church, Augusta, Georgia, September 11, 1864.* Augusta, GA: Jas. Nathan Ells, Publisher, Baptist Banner Office, 1864.

Burrows, J. L. *The New Richmond Theatre. A Discourse Delivered on Sunday, February 8, 1863, in the First Baptist Church, Richmond, VA.* Richmond: Smith, Bailey & Co., 1862.

Butler, William C. *Sermon Preached in St. John's Church, Richmond, Virginia, on the Sunday After the Battle of Manassas, July 21, 1861, by the Rector.* Richmond: Chas. A. Wynne, Printer, 1861.

Carlisle, John S. Speech in the Virginia State Convention, March 7, 1861, in Frank Moore, ed. *The Rebellion Record: A Diary of American Events with Documents, Narratives, Illustrative Incidents, Poetry, Etc.* Supplement Vol. 1. New York: D. Van Nostrand, 1866.

Chambers, H[enry] C. (Hon.). Policy of Employing Negro Troops. Speech of Hon. H. C. Chambers, of Mississippi, in the House of Representatives of the Congress of the Confederate States, Thursday, November 10, 1864, on the special order for that day, being the resolution offered by him on the first day of the session . . . n.p., n.d.

Clark, B. M. See C. Sidney Lobdell.

Cobb, Howell. Speech at Atlanta, Georgia, January 28, 1864. In Frank Moore, ed. *The Rebellion Record: A Diary of American Events, with Documents, Narratives, Illustrative Incidents, Poetry, Etc.* Vol. 8. New York: D. Van Nostrand, 1867.

_____. Speech at Atlanta, Georgia, May 22, 1861. In *Echoes from the South. Comprising the Most Important Speeches, Proclamations, and Public Acts Emanating from the South during the Late War.* New York: E. B. Treat & Co., 1866.

_____. Speech at Atlanta, Georgia, May 29(?), 1861. In *Milledgeville Federal Union*, June 4, 1861.

Cobb, T[homas] R. R. Substance of an Address of T. R. R. Cobb to his Constituents of Clark County, location unknown, April 6, 1861. n. p., n. d.

Collier, R. R. *Remarks on the Subject of the Ownership of Slaves, Delivered by R. R. Collier of Petersburg, in the Senate of Virginia,* October, 12, 1863. Richmond: James E. Goode, 1863.

Dalzell, W. T. D. (Rev.). *Thanksgiving to God. A Sermon Preached in St. Mark's Church, San Antonio. On Wednesday, 4th Feb., 1863.* San Antonio: Herald Book and Job Press, n. d.

Davis, Jefferson. Speech at Montgomery, Alabama, February 16, 1861. In *Charleston Mercury,* February 18, 1861.

Davis, Jefferson, Henry Wise. Speeches at Public Meeting, location obscured, date obscured [Richmond, June 1, 1861]. In *Milledgeville Federal Union,* June 11, 1861.

DeJarnette, Daniel. "The Monroe Doctrine." Speech of Hon. D. C. DeJarnette, of Virginia, in the Confederate House of Representatives, January 30, 1865, Pending Negotiations for Peace. n.p., n. d.

Desaussure, Henry, George S. Bryan, Nelson Mitchell, David Ramsay, Robert Rhett, Richard Yeadon. Remarks on the death of James L. Pettigrew, delivered at the meeting of the Charleston Bar, March 25, 1863. In *Charleston Mercury,* April 20, 1863.

Devine, Thos. J. (Hon.) and Hon. A. W. Terrell. *Speeches Delivered on the 17th January, 1862 in the Representative Hall, Austin, Texas.* Austin: John Marshall & Co., 1862.

Dick, Robert. Substance of remarks made on the motion to adjourn the North Carolina Convention, date unknown. In *North Carolina Standard,* May 14, 1862.

Doggett, D. S. (Pastor).*The War and Its Close. A Discourse Delivered in Centenary Church, Richmond, Va., Friday, April 8, 1864, on the Occasion of the National Fast.* Richmond: Macfarlane & Fergusson, 1864.

Doggett, D. S. (Rev.). *A Nation's Ebenezer. A Discourse Delivered in the Broad St. Methodist Church, Richmond, Virginia, Thursday, September 18, 1862: The Day of Public Thanksgiving, Appointed by the president of the Confederate States.* Richmond: Enquirer Book and Job Press, 1862.

Echols, Joseph. Speech in Confederate House of Representatives, January 19, 1865, in opposition to a motion to recommit a bill to seize all the cotton and tobacco of the Confederacy. n.p., n. d.

Elliott, Stephen (Rt. Rev.). *Our Cause in Harmony with the Purposes of God in Christ Jesus. A Sermon Preached in Christ Church, Savannah, on Thursday, September 18, 1862, Being the Day Set Forth by the President of the Confederate States, as a Day of Prayer and Thanksgiving, for Our Manifold Victories, and Especially for the Fields of Manassas and Richmond, Ky. By the Rt. Rev. Stephen Elliott, D. D., Rector of Christ Church, and Bishop of the Diocese of Georgia.* Savannah: Power Press of John M. Cooper & Co., 1862.

Elliott, Stephen (Rev.). *How to Renew our National Strength, Sermon at Christ Church, Savannah, Georgia, November 15, 1861, on the day of Humiliation, Fasting and Prayer.* Richmond: Macfarlane & Fergusson Printers, 1862.

Elliott, Stephen (Rt. Rev.). *Ezra's Dilemma. A Sermon Preached in Christ Church, Savannah, on Friday, August 21, 1863, Being the Day of Humiliation, Fasting and Prayer, Appointed by the President of the Confederate States, by the Rt. Rev. Stephen Elliott, D. D., Rector of Christ Church, and the Bishop of the Diocese of Georgia.* Savannah, Georgia: Power Press of George N. Nichols, 1863.

Elliot, Stephen (Rt. Rev.). *The Silver Trumpets of the Sanctuary, A Sermon Preached to The Pulaski Guards in Christ Church, Savannah, on the Second Sunday after Trinity, Being the Sunday Before Their Departure to Join the Army in Virginia, by the Rt. Rev. Stephen Elliott, D. D., Rector of Christ Church.* Savannah: Steam Press of John M. Cooper & Company, 1861.

Elliott, Stephen (Rt. Rev.). *"Vain is the Help of Man." A Sermon Preached in Christ Church, Savannah, on Thursday, September 15, 1864, Being the Day of Fasting, Humiliation, and Prayer, Appointed by the Governor of the State of Georgia.* Macon, GA: Burke, Boykin & Company, 1864.

Ennett, W. T. (Maj.). Speech at Turkey Creek School House, North Carolina, September 17, 1864. In *Wilmington Journal Weekly*, October 27, 1864.

Fenston, (Col.). See John Baldwin.

Finley, I. R. (Rev.). *The Lord Reigneth: A Sermon Preached in Lloyd's Church, Sussex County, Va., Sunday August 16, 1863.* Richmond: Soldiers Tract Association, M. E. Church South. Chas. Wynne, Printer, n. d.

Fisher, Dr. N. Speech before the Wilkinson Rifle Company, date unknown. In *Milledgeville Federal Union*, May 7, 1861.

Foote, Henry, Jabez Curry. Remarks in the debate on the bill for the burning of cotton, tobacco, and other property, in Confederate House of Representatives, March 5, 1862. Paraphrase. *Southern Historical Society Papers.* vol. 44. Richmond: Southern Historical Society, 1923; reprint, Broadfoot Publishing Company, 1991.

Foote, Henry. Remarks on his resolution, delivered in the Confederate House of Representatives, November 9, 1864 (paraphrase), in "Proceedings of the Second Confederate Congress, Second Session in Part, 7 November–14 November, 1864," in Frank E. Vandiver, ed., *Southern Historical Society Papers.* vol. 51. Richmond: The Virginia Historical Society, 1958; reprint, Broadfoot Publishing, 1992.

Gaither, Mr. Remarks on the proposition to extend the Conscription Laws, delivered in the Confederate House of Representatives, August 23, 1862. In *North Carolina Standard*, September 3, 1862.

Gantt, E. W. (Brig. Gen.). *Address.* Little Rock: n.p., 1863. University Archives, Howard-Tilton Memorial Library, Tulane University, New Orleans.

Gholson, Thomas. *Speech of Hon. Thomas S. Gholson, of Virginia, on the Policy of Employing Negro Troops, and the Duty of All Classes to Aid in the Prosecution of the War, Delivered in the House of Representatives of the Congress of the Confederate States, on the 1st of February, 1865.* Richmond: George P. Evans & Co., Printers, 1865.

Gierlow, J. (Rev.) Sermon. A View of the Present Crisis, by Rev. J. Gierlow, Rector of St. James Church. Baton Rouge, Louisiana, August, 1861. n. p., n. d. Source unknown.

Gierlow, (Rev.) Fast-Day Sermon. Extract. Date unknown, location unknown. In *Baton Rouge Weekly Gazette and Comet,* December 5, 1861.

Gilmer, John A. (Hon.). Speech of Hon. John A. Gilmer, of North Carolina, in the United States House of Representatives, January 26, 1861. In *Hillsborough Recorder*, February 13, 1861.

_____. See also Robert Mercer Hunter.

Goode, John B. (Hon.). See John Baldwin.

Gordon, George. Speech of Hon. George Gordon, of Chatham, on the Constitutionality of the Conscription Laws Passed by the Congress of the Confederate States, Delivered in the Senate of Georgia on Tuesday, 9th December, 1862. N. p., n. d.

Graham, W. A. Remarks on the Message of the Governor touching on the case of R. J. Graves, delivered in the Senate of North Carolina,

January 22, 1863. In *Hillsborough Recorder*, February 4, 1863.

Graham, W. A. State of the Country Address at Hillsborough, North Carolina militia meeting, April, 1861. In *Hillsborough Recorder*, May, 1861.

Gregg, Alexander. (Rt. Rev.). *A Sermon preached in St. David's Church, Austin, on Sunday, March 15th, 1863*. By the Rt. Rev. Alexander Gregg, D. D., Bishop of the Diocese of Texas. Texas Almanac Office, 1863.

Hall, Samuel. Remarks of the Commissioner from Georgia before the General Assembly of North Carolina, February 13, 1861. In *Wilmington Journal Weekly*, February 14, 1861.

Grissom, Mr. Remarks upon the adoption of the Majority Resolutions in relation to *Habeas Corpus*, delivered in North Carolina House of Commons, May 25, 1864. In *North Carolina Standard*, June 1, 1864.

Hall, Samuel. Remarks of the Commissioner from Georgia before the General Assembly of North Carolina, February 13, 1861. In *Wilmington Journal Weekly*, February 14, 1861.

Hammond, Samuel L. See A. P. Lining.

Henry, Gustavus A. Speech of the Hon. Gustavus A. Henry, of Tennessee, on his joint resolution, defining the position of the Confederate States, and declaring the determination of the Congress and the people thereof to prosecute the war till their independence is acknowledged, delivered in the Confederate Senate, November 29, 1864. n.p., n.d.
_____. See also Robert Mercer Hunter.

Higgins, S. H. (Rev.). *"The Mountain Moved; or David upon the Cause and Cure of Public Calamity." Sermon By Rev. S. H. Higgins, D.D. Delivered on Fast Day in Milledgeville, December 10th, 1864*. At the Request of the General Assembly of Georgia. Excerpt. Milledgeville, GA: Boughton, Nisbet, Barnes & Moore, State Printers, 1863.

Hill, Benjamin H. Remarks in Confederate Senate against motion to take up the House exemption bill, February 12, 1863, paraphrase. In *Southern Historical Papers*. Vol. 48. Richmond: 1941; reprint, Broadfoot Publishing Company, Morningside Bookshop, 1992.
_____. Speech Delivered at La Grange, Ga., March 11, 1865. In Benjamin H. Hill, Jr. *Senator Benjamin H. Hill of Georgia, His Life, Speeches, and Writings*. Atlanta: T. H. P. Bloodworth, 1893.
_____. Speech delivered before the Georgia Legislature, in Milledgeville, December 11, 1862. In Benjamin H. Hill, Jr. *Senator Benjamin H. Hill of Georgia, His Life, Speeches, and Writings*. Atlanta: T. H. P. Bloodworth, 1893.

Hoge, Rev. Dr. See Robert Mercer Hunter.

Houston, Sam. Speech at Houston, March 18, 1863. In *Memphis Daily Appeal*, April 16, 1863.

Houston, Sam. Speech at Independence, Texas, May 10, 1861. In *Echoes from the South, Comprising the Most Important Speeches, Proclamations, and Public Acts Emanating from the South during the Late War*. New York: E. B. Treat & Co., 1866.

Hunter, R[obert] M[ercer] T[aliaferro] (Rev.), Mr. Sheffey, Hon. J[udah] P. Benjamin, Hon. John A. Gilmer, Senator T[homas] J[enkins] Semmes, Senator Gustavus A. Henry, J. Randolph Tucker, Rev. Dr. Hoge. Speeches and sketches of speeches delivered at the mass meeting at the African Church, Richmond, Virginia, February 9, 1865. In *Richmond Daily Enquirer*, February 10, 1865 and February 13, 1865.

Jacobs, Ferdinand (Rev.). *A Sermon, for the Times: Preached in Fairview Presbyterian Church, Perry County, Alabama on Thursday, June 13, 1861–The Day of Fasting and Prayer, appointed by the Confederate Authorities, in View of the National Exigencies*. Published by request of the Congregation, Marion, AL, 1861.

Jones, C. C. (Rev.). *Religious Instruction of the Negroes. An Address delivered before the General Assembly of the Presbyterian Church, at Augusta, Ga, December 10, 1861*. Richmond: Presbyterian Committee of Publication. n. d.

Jones, J. (Rev.). *The Southern Soldier's Duty. A Discourse Delivered By Rev. J. Jones to the Rome Light Guards and Miller Rifles in The Presbyterian Church of Rome, Ga., on Sabbath Morning, the 26th of May, 1861*. Excerpt. Rome: Power Press of D. H. Mason, 1881.

Jumper, John (Col.). Speech to the Creeks and Seminoles comprising the 1st Seminole Regiment, delivered at Camp Limestone Prairie, Indian Territory, July 6, 1864. N. p., n. d. Printed at government Printing Office, Ft. Towson, CT, July 21st, 1864.

Keitt, L. M. Speech at the Serenade to Hon. Alexander Stephens, Montgomery, Alabama, February 7, 1861. In *Charleston Mercury*, February 11, 18, 1861.

King, T. Butler (Hon.). *Speech of the Hon. T. Butler King, Delivered in the Hall of the House of Representatives, at Milledgeville, GA, November 10, 1863*. Milledgeville, GA: Boughton, Nisbet, Barnes & Moore, State Printers, 1863.

Lamar, Lucius. The State of the Country at Home and Abroad. Address delivered at the Atheneum, Atlanta, Ga., April 14, 1864. In Edward Mayes. *Lucius Q. C. Lamar: His Life, Times, and Speeches, 1825–1893*.

Nashville: Publishing House of the Methodist Episcopal Church South. Barbee and Smith, Agents, 1896.

Lining, A. P., Lt. J. A. Blake, M. P. O'Conner, Esq., and Samuel L. Hammond. Speeches at Fourth of July Celebration, Charleston, South Carolina, July 4, 1861. In *Charleston Daily Courier*, July 6, 1861.

Lobdell, C. Sidney, B. M. Clark. Speeches at the Flag Presentation to the Delta Rifles, Baton Rouge, Louisiana, delivered April 20, 1861. In *West Baton Rouge Sugar Planter*, April 27, 1861.

Marshall, H[umphrey] (Hon.). Sketch of the Remarks of Honorable H. Marshall, of Kentucky, made in the House of Representatives of the Confederate States Congress, 15th January, 1865. In *Richmond Whig*, January 23, 1865.

Marshall, Mr. [Humphrey]. Sketch of remarks on the Tax Bill, delivered in the Confederate House of Representatives, February 21, 1865. In *Richmond Whig*, February 23, 1865.

Mason, J[ames] M[urray]. Speech at Richmond, Virginia, June 8, 1861. In *Echoes from the South, Comprising the Most Important Speeches, Proclamations, and Public Acts Emanating from the South during the Late War*. New York: E. B. Treat & Co., 1866.

McKay, W. Speech before the Macon Commercial Convention, Macon, Georgia, October 16, 1861. In *Charleston Daily Courier*, October 26, 1861.

Miles, James Warley (Rev.). God in History. Extract from a discourse delivered before the graduating class of the College of Charleston, Sunday evening, March 29, 1863. In *Hillsborough Recorder*, May 20, 1863.

Minnigerode, Charles (Rev.). *"He that believeth shall not make haste": A Sermon Preached on the First of January, 1865, in St. Paul's Church, Richmond*. Richmond: Charles H. Wynne, Publisher, 1865.

_____. *Power: A Sermon Preached at St. Paul's Church, Richmond, on the 13th November, 1864*. Richmond: W. H. Clement, Book and Job Printers, 1864.

Muller, L. (Rev.). Sermon at Institute Hall, on Fast Day, June 13, 1861, Delivered before the German Military Companies and German Population, Charleston, South Carolina. In *Charleston Daily Courier*, June 17, 1861.

Murray, John P. (Hon.). Speech of Hon. John P. Murray, of Tennessee, in favor of repealing the act suspending the privilege of the writ of *habeas corpus*, date unknown, 1864? N. p., n. d.

Nelson, T. A. R. Address to the people of East Tennessee, date unknown, location unknown. In *Memphis Daily Appeal*, October, 11, 1862.

O'Connor, M. P. See A. P. Lining.

Oldham, William. Speech of Hon. W. S. Oldham, of Texas, on the
Resolutions of the State of Texas, concerning Peace, Reconstruction,
and Independence, delivered in the Confederate Senate, January 30,
1865. N. p., n. d. Center for Study of American History, The University
of Texas, Austin, Texas.

Oldham, William. Speech of W. S. Oldham, of Texas, upon the Bill to
Amend the Conscript Law, made in the Confederate Senate,
September 4, 1862. N. p., n. d.

Palmer, B. M. (Rev.). Address at the funeral of General Maxey Gregg,
delivered in the Presbyterian Church, Columbia, South Carolina,
December 20, 1862. In *Columbia Guardian*, January 28, 1863, in South
Caroliniana Library, Columbia, South Carolina.

Palmer, Dr. (Rev.). Speech at a barbeque for soldiers of Hampton's
Legion, delivered in Columbia, South Carolina, April, 1864. In
Montgomery Daily Advertiser, May 5, 1864.

Parks, John (Rev.). *Sermon before Brigadier-General Hoke's Brigade upon
the Execution of 22 men for Desertion, 28 February 1864, at Kingston,
North Carolina.* Greensborough, North Carolina: A. W. Lincoln & Co.,
Book and Job Printers, 1864.

Perkins, John. Remarks of Hon. John Perkins, of Louisiana, on
presenting from the Committee on Foreign Affairs, Resolutions in
regard to the Negotiations for Peace, delivered in the Confederate
House of Representatives, exact date unknown, 1865. N.p., n.d.

Perkins, Mr. Remarks of Mr. Perkins, of Louisiana, in the Confederate
House of Representatives, May 3, 1864. N. p., n. d.

Phelan, James (Hon.). Speech of Hon. James Phelan of Mississippi on
the Judiciary Bill delivered in the Confederate Senate, exact date
unknown, 1862? N. p., n. d.

Phelan, James (Hon.). *Speech of Hon. James Phelan, of Mississippi, on the
Motion to Conscript "Justices of the Peace," and Involving the Power of
Congress to Exact Military Service of a State Officer, Delivered in the
Senate of the Confederate States, September 6, 1862.* Richmond:
Enquirer Book and Job Press, 1862.

Pickens, Francis (Gov.). Speech at Charleston, South Carolina, April
14(?), 1861. In *Charleston Daily Courier*, April 15, 1861.

Pierce, Reverend H. N. *Sermons Preached in St. John's Church, Mobile,
Alabama, on the 13th of June, 1861, The National Fast, Appointed by His
Excellency Jefferson Davis, President of the Confederate States of
America.* Mobile: Farrow & Bennett, Book and Job Printers, 1861.

Price, Sterling (Gen.). Speech to soldiers at Port Hudson, date unknown. In *Wilmington Daily Journal*, April 9, 1863.

Pryor, Roger. Speech at Charleston, April 10, 1861. In *Charleston Daily Courier*, April 11, 1861.

Raiford, Hon. E. G. Remarks in Georgia House of Representatives, December 14, 1861. In *Georgia Weekly Telegraph*, December 20, 1861.

Randolph, Reverend A. M. *Address on the Day of Fasting and Prayer Appointed by the President of the Confederate States, June 13, 1861, Delivered in St. George's Church, Fredericksburg, Virginia.* Fredericksburg: The Recorder Job Office, 1861.

Raymond, H. R. *A Sermon With Reference to the Death of David Y. Huntington, Who Fell on Manassas Plains 20th August, 1862.* Preached in The Presbyterian Church, Marion, Alabama, on the 8th February, 1863. Published by the Parents. Marion, AL: George C. Rogers, Printers, 1863.

Read, Mr. [Edwin]. Remarks in the Confederate Senate, January 30, 1864. In Frank E. Vandiver, ed., "Proceedings of the First Confederate Congress, Fourth Session, 7 December, 1863–18 February, 1864. *Southern Historical Society Papers.* Vol. 50. Richmond: The Virginia Historical Society, 1953.

Renfroe, J. J. D. *"The Battle is God's": A Sermon Preached Before Wilcox's Brigade on Fast Day, the 21st August, 1863,* Near Orange Court-House, Virginia, by J. J. D. Renfroe, Chaplain 10th Alabama Regiment. Richmond: MacFarlane & Fergusson, 1863.

Rhett, R[obert] B[arnwell], Mr. Barnwell. Speeches in the South Carolina State Convention, September 14, 1862. In *Charleston Daily Courier,* October 2, 1862.

Rice, Thomas O. (Rev.). Address Before the South Carolina Sunday School Union at their Forty-Second Anniversary, Charleston, South Carolina, May 12, 1861. In *Charleston Daily Courier,* May 16, 1861.

Rivers, Professor William. Address of Professor Wm. J. Rivers of the South Carolina College, delivered Before the South Carolina Historical Society, delivered at Hibernian Hall, Charleston, South Carolina, May 14, 1861. In *Charleston Daily Courier,* May 15, 1861.

Russell, Charles W. Graduation address before the Richmond Medical College, date unknown. In *Richmond Enquirer,* March 28, 1862.

_____. Speech of Hon. Charles Russell of Virginia, on Retaliation, delivered in the Confederate House of Representatives, October 1, 1862. In *Richmond Enquirer,* October 10, 1862.

Semmes, Thomas Jenkins. See Robert Mercer Hunter.

Sheffey, Mr. See Robert Mercer Hunter.

Simms, W. E. Speech of Hon. W. E. Simms of Kentucky, in reply to Mr.
Yancey upon the Amendment to the Exemption bill, proposed by Mr.
Dortch, that Justices of the Peace should be Liable to Conscription.
Delivered in the Senate of the Confederate States, September 15, 1862.
In *Richmond Enquirer*, January 10, 1863.

Simons, James (Gen.), Sergeant Welch. Speeches at The Eighty-Fifth
Anniversary of the Battle of Fort Moultrie, Charleston, South
Carolina, June 28, 1861. In *Charleston Daily Courier*, June 29, 1861.

Smith, Governor. Speech on the condition of the country, to the citizens
of Petersburg, Virginia, November 4, 1863. Partial Paraphrase. In
Hillsborough Recorder, November 11, 1863.

Smith, Mr. Remarks of Mr. Smith, of Macon, on the Ordinance to
prohibit, for a limited time, the manufacture of Spirituous Liquors,
delivered in the North Carolina Convention, date unknown. In *North
Carolina Standard*, March 5, 1862.

Smith, Robert H. *An Address to the Citizens of Alabama, on the
Constitution and Laws of the Confederate States of America, by the
Hon. Robert H. Smith, at Temperance Hall, on the 30th day of March,
1861*. Mobile: Mobile Daily Register Print, 1861.

Speaker unknown. Science and Religion Not At Variance.
Commencement Oration, delivered at the Annual Commencement of
the College of Charleston, March 1862. In *Charleston Daily Courier*,
August 26, 1862.

Staples, Walter. Remarks of Walter Staples, of Montgomery, on the
Death of William Ballard Preston, delivered in the Confederate
House of Representatives, January 16, 1863. In *Richmond Enquirer*,
January 20, 1863.

Stephens, Alexander. Speech in Savannah, Georgia, delivered on March
21, 1861, known as "The Corner Stone Speech," reported in the
Savannah Republican. In Henry Cleveland. *Alexander Stephens, in
Public and Private. With Letters and Speeches before, during, and since
the War*. Philadelphia: National Publishing Co., 1866.

_____. Speech at Augusta, Georgia, delivered July 11, 1861, in Frank
Moore, ed. *The Rebellion Record: A Diary of American Events with
Documents, Narratives, Illustrative Incidents, Poetry, Etc.* Vol. 2. New
York: D. Van Nostrand, 1866.

_____. Synopsis of the Substance of Address at Crawfordville, Georgia,

November 1, 1862. Reported by J. Henley Smith. In Henry Cleveland. *Alexander Stephens in Public and Private. With Letters and Speeches before, during, and Since the War.* Philadelphia: National Publication Co., 1866.Terrell, Hon. A. W. *Oration Delivered on the Fourth Day of July, 1861, at the Capitol, Austin, Texas.* Austin: John Marshall & Co., 1861.

Swan, W. G. *Foreign Relations. Speech of Hon. W. G. Swan, of Tennessee, Delivered in the House of Representatives of the Confederate States, February 5, 1863 .* Richmond: Smith, Bailey & Co., Printers, 1863.

Terrell, A. W. (Hon.). *Oration Delivered on the Fourth Day of July, 1861, at the Capitol, Austin, Texas.* Austin: John Marshall & Co., 1861.

_____. See also Thos. J. Devine.

Thomas, Colonel. Speech at camp near Centreville, Virginia, October 17, 1861. In *Wilmington Daily Journal,* November 7, 1861.

Toombs, Robert. Speech in the Georgia House of Representatives, extract, November 9, 1863. In *Memphis Daily Appeal,* November 13, 1863.

Tucker, J. Randolph. See Robert Mercer Taliaferro.

Tucker, J. V.(?) (Rev.). *The Guilt and Punishment of Extortion: A Sermon Preached by Rev. J. V. Tucker, Before his Congregation in Fayetteville, on Sunday, the 7th of September, 1862.* Fayetteville, NC: The Presbyterian Office, 1862.

Tupper, H. A. (Rev.). *A Thanksgiving Discourse, Delivered at Washington, Ga., on Thursday, September 18, 1862.* Macon, GA: Burke, Boykin & Co., Steam Book and Job Printers, 1862.Turner, Josiah. Speech of Col. Thomas of the 15th Regiment Georgia Volunteers, at Hillsborough, North Carolina, April 20, 1861, partial paraphrase. In *Hillsborough Recorder,* April 24, 1861.

Turner, Josiah (Hon.). Remarks of Hon. Josiah Turner, of North Carolina, on the Resolutions Proposing Negotiations for Peace with the Enemy, delivered in Confederate Congress, date unknown. In *Hillsborough Recorder,* January 4, 1865.

Vance, Governor Zebulon B. Inaugural Address, delivered in Raleigh, North Carolina, September 8, 1862. In *Wilmington Journal Weekly,* September 18, 1862.

_____. Sketch of speech at the Public Meeting at Goldsboro, North Carolina on Saturday, February 18, 1865. In *Richmond Whig,* February 23, 1865.

_____. Speech on Washington's Birthday, delivered to citizens of Wilkes

County, at Hillsborough(?), North Carolina, February 22, 1864. In *Hillsborough Recorder*, March 9, 1864, and March 16, 1864.

Watkins, W. H. (Rev.). The South, Her Position and Duty. A Discourse Delivered at the Methodist Church, Natchez, Mississippi, January 4, 1861. N. p., n. d., in Mississippi Department of Archives and History, Jackson, Mississippi.

Watts, [Thomas] (Gov.). Synopsis of remarks before the Mass Meeting, held in Montgomery, on February 25, 1865. In *Montgomery Daily Advertiser*, March 3, 1865.

Welch, (Sergeant). See General James Simons.

Wheelwright, Wm. H. (Rev.). *A Discourse Delivered to the Troops, Stationed at Glouchester Point, VA., February 28ᵗʰ, 1862. By the Rev. Wm. H. Wheelwright.* Richmond: Chas. H. Wynne, Printer, 1862.

Wigfall, Mr. Remarks of Mr. Wigfall of Texas, on the Exemption Bill, delivered in Confederate Senate, February 12, 1863. *Southern Historical Society Papers.* vol. 48. Richmond: Southern Historical Society, 1941; reprint Broadfoot Publishing Company, 1992.

Wigfall, L. T. Speech at Charleston, April 3, 1861. In *Montgomery Daily Advertiser*, April 6, 1861.

Winkler, E. T. (Rev.). *Duties of the Citizen Soldier. A Sermon Delivered in the First Baptist Church of Charleston, S.C., on Sabbath Morning, January 6, 1861, before the Moultrie Guards. By E. T. Winkler, Chaplain of the Company.* Charleston: A. J. Burke, 1861.

Wise, Henry A. Speech in spring, 1861, date unknown, location unknown. [Richmond, June 1, 1861] In *Echoes from the South, Comprising the Most Important Speeches, Proclamations, and Public Acts Emanating from the South during the Late War.* (New York: E. B. Treat & Co., 1866).

Yancey, William. Speech on retaliation, delivered in the Confederate Senate, August 21, 1862. N. p., n. d.

_____. Speech on the Appointment of Brigadier Generals, delivered in the Confederate Senate, September 22, 1862. N. p., n. d.

Yeadon, Richard. A Lecture on Gunboats. Address before the Ladies' Soldiers' Relief Association, Aiken, South Carolina, March 12, 1862. In *Charleston Daily Courier*, March 19, 1862.

_____. The Garden and the Vineyard. Anniversary Address before the Aiken Vine-Growing and Horticultural Association, date unknown. In *Charleston Daily Courier*, August 30, 1862.

SELECTED SOURCES

Articles

Bitzer, Lloyd F. "The Rhetorical Situation." *Philosophy and Rhetoric* 1 (1968): 1–14.

Bormann, Ernest G. "Fantasy and Rhetorical Vision: The Rhetorical Criticism of Social Reality." *Quarterly Journal of Speech* 58 (1972): 396–407.

Campbell, John Angus. "Special Issue of Rhetorical Criticism: Introduction." *Western Journal of Speech Communication* 54 (Summer, 1990): 249–51.

Campbell, Kathryn Kohrs. "Gender and Genre: Loci of Invention and Contradiction in the Earliest Speeches of U. S. Women." *The Quarterly Journal of Speech* 81 (1995): 479–95.

Henry, David. "The Rhetorical Dynamics of Mario Cuomo's 1984 Keynote Address: Situation, Speaker, and Metaphor." *Southern Speech Communication Journal* 53 (Winter, 1988): 105–20.

Henseley, Carl Wayne. "Rhetorical Vision and the Persuasion, A Historical Movement: The Disciples of Christ in Nineteenth-Century American Culture." *Quarterly Journal of Speech* 61 (1975): 250–64.

Lebergott, Stanley. "Why the South Lost: Commercial Purpose in the Confederacy, 1861–1865." *Journal of American History* 70 (June, 1983): 58–74.

Leff, Michael. "Things Made by Words: Reflections of Textual Criticism." *The Quarterly Journal of Speech* 78 (1992): 223–31.

_____. "Topical Invention and Metaphoric Interaction." *Southern Speech Communication Journal* 48 (Spring, 1983): 214–29.

Leff, Michael, and Andrew Sachs. "Words the Most Like Things: Iconicity and the Rhetorical Text." *Western Journal of Speech Communication* 54 (Summer, 1990): 252–73.

McGee, Michael Calvin. "Text, Context, and the Fragmentation of Contemporary Culture." *Western Journal of Speech Communication* 54 (Summer, 1990): 274–89.

Olson, Kathryn M. "The Controversy over President Reagan's Visit to Bitburg: Strategies of Definition and Redefinition." *The Quarterly Journal of Speech* 75 (1989): 129–51.

Pessen, Edward. "How Different from Each Other Were Antebellum North and South?" *American Historical Review* 85 (December, 1980): 1119–49.

Peterson, Owen M. "The South in the Democratic National Convention of 1860." *Southern Speech Journal* 20 (Winter, 1954): 212–23.

Richardson, Ralph. "The Rhetorical Death Rattle of the Confederacy." *Southern Speech Journal* 20 (Winter, 1954): 109–17.

Silver, James W. "Propaganda in the Confederacy." *Journal of Southern History* 11 (November, 1945): 487–503.

Books

Aiken, South Carolina: A Description of the Climate, Soils, and the Nature of the Products in the Vicinity of Aiken, South Carolina, Especially Fruit, Cereals, Cotton, Corn, etc. Including Extracts from Letters of Distinguished Visitors, Correspondents, Action of Town Councils Inviting Emigrants, etc., etc. New York: J. C. Derby, Pub., 1870.

Akin, Warren. *Letters of Warren Akin: Confederate Congressman.* Ed. Bell Irvin Wiley. Athens: University of Georgia Press, 1959.

Ash, Stephen V. *Middle Tennessee Society Transformed, 1860–1870: War and Peace in the Upper South.* Baton Rouge and London: Louisiana State University Press, 1988.

_____. *When the Yankees Came: Conflict and Chaos in the Occupied South, 1861–1865.* Chapel Hill and London: The University of North Carolina Press, 1995.

Bakker, Jan. *Pastoral in Antebellum Southern Romance.* Southern Literary Studies. Baton Rouge and London: Louisiana State University Press, 1989.

Barton, Michael. *Goodmen: The Character of Civil War Soldiers.* University Park and London: The Pennsylvania State University Press, 1981.

Beringer, Richard E., Herman Hathaway, Archer Jones, William N. Still, Jr. *Why the South Lost the Civil War.* Athens and London: University of Georgia Press, 1986.

Berkeley, Henry Robinson. *Four Years in the Confederate Artillery: The Diary of Private Henry Robinson Berkeley.* Ed. William H. Runge. Chapel Hill: University of North Carolina Press, 1961.

Bettersworth, John K., ed. *Mississippi in the Confederacy as they saw it.* Published for Mississippi Department of Archives and History, Jackson, Mississippi. Baton Rouge: Louisiana State University Press, 1961.

Braden, Waldo W., ed., with the assistance of J. Jeffery Auer and Bert E. Bradley. *Oratory in the Old South: 1828–1860.* Baton Rouge and

London: Louisiana State University Press, 1970.

_____. *The Oral Tradition in the South.* Baton Rouge: Louisiana State University Press: 1983.

Bryan, T. Conn. *Confederate Georgia.* Athens: University of Georgia Press, 1953.

Burke, Kenneth. *On Symbols and Society.* Edited and with an Introduction by Joseph R. Gusfield. The Heritage of Society Series. Ed. Donald Lezine. Chicago: The University of Chicago Press, 1989.

Campbell, Karlyn Kohrs and Kathleen Hall Jamieson, eds. *Form and Genre: Shaping Rhetorical Action.* Edited and with an introductory essay by Karlyn Kohrs Campbell and Kathleen Hall Jamieson. Falls Church, VA: The Speech Communication Association, 1974.

Cantrill, James G. and Christine L. Oravec, eds. *The Symbolic Earth: Discourse and Our Creation of the Environment.* Lexington: The University Press of Kentucky, 1996.

Cash, William J. *The Mind of the South.* New York: Knopf, 1941.

Cassidy, Vincent H. and Amos E. Simpson. *Henry Watkins Allen of Louisiana.* Baton Rouge: Louisiana State University Press, 1964.

Chambers, Henry A. *Diary of Captain Henry A. Chambers.* Ed. T. H. Pearce. Wendell, NC: Broadfoot's Bookmark, 1983.

Chesnut, Mary B. *A Diary from Dixie.* Ed. Ben Ames Williams. With a Foreword by Edmund Wilson. Boston: Houghton Mifflin, 1949; reprint, Cambridge, MA: Harvard University Press, 1980.

Cleveland, Henry. *Alexander Stephens in Public and Private. With Letters and Speeches Before, During, and Since the War.* Philadelphia: National Publishing Co., 1866.

Coleman, Kenneth. *Confederate Athens.* Athens: University of Georgia Press, 1967.

Confederate Imprints, 1861–1865: Based on Crandall, Marjorie Lyle, Confederate Imprints, 1955 and Harwell, Richard B., More Confederate Imprints, 1957. Woodbridge, CN: Research Publications, 1974. Microfilm Reels. Reel Index edited by Edward A. Reno, Jr., and Margaret M. Brezicki. New Haven, CT: Research Publications, Inc., 1974.

Connelly, Thomas Lawrence. *Army of the Heartland: The Army of Tennessee, 1861–1862.* Baton Rouge: Louisiana State University Press, 1967.

Connelly, Thomas, and Archer Jones. *The Politics of Command: Factions and Ideas in Confederate Strategy.* Baton Rouge: Louisiana State University Press, 1973.

Conolly, Thomas. *An Irishman in Dixie: Thomas Conolly's Diary of the Fall of the Confederacy.* First Edition. Ed. by Nelson D. Lankford. Columbia: University of South Carolina Press, 1988.

Cooper, William J., Jr. *The South and the Politics of Slavery: 1828–1856.* Baton Rouge and London: Louisiana State University Press, 1978.

Corbett, Edward P. J. *Classical Rhetoric for the Modern Student.* 3d ed. New York and Oxford: Oxford University Press, 1990.

Cowdrey, Albert E. *This Land, This South: An Environmental History.* New Perspectives on the South Series. Lexington: The University Press of Kentucky, 1983.

Crandall, Marjorie Lyle. *Confederate Imprints: A Check List Based Principally on the Collection of the Boston Athenaeum.* With an introduction by Walter Muir Whitehill. 2 Vols. Portland, ME: The Athenaeum Press, 1955.

Culpepper, Marilyn Mayer. *Trials and Triumphs: Women of the American Civil War.* East Lansing: Michigan State University Press, 1991.

Cumming, Kate. *Kate: The Journal of a Confederate Nurse.* Ed. Richard Barksdale Harwell. Baton Rouge: Louisiana State University Press, 1959.

Curti, Merle. *The Growth of American Thought.* 3d. ed. New York and London: Harper and Row, Publishers, 1964.

Daniel, John M. *The Richmond Examiner During the War, or, The Writings of John M. Daniel.* The American Journalist Series. n.p.: Arno Press, Inc., 1970.

Daniel, Larry J. *Soldiering in the Army of Tennessee: A Portrait of Life in a Confederate Army.* Chapel Hill and London: The University of North Carolina Press, 1991.

Davis, Jefferson. *The Rise and Fall of the Confederate Government.* 2 vols. New York: D. Appleton and Co., 1881.

Dawson, Francis W. *Reminiscences of Confederate Service: 1860–1865.* Ed. Bell I. Wiley, with an introduction, Appendix, and notes. Library of Southern Civilization, Lewis P. Simpson, Editor. Baton Rouge and London: Louisiana State University Press, 1980.

Dorsey, Sarah A. *Recollections of Henry Watkins Allen: Brigadier-General Confederate States Army, Ex-Governor of Louisiana.* New York: M. Doolady, 1866.

Duffy, Bernard K. and Halford R. Ryan, eds. *American Orators Before 1900: Critical Studies and Sources.* New York and Westport, CN: Greenwood Press, 1987.

Durden, Robert F. *The Gray and the Black: The Confederate Debate On*

Emancipation. Baton Rouge: Louisiana State University Press, 1972.

Eaton, Clement. *A History of the Southern Confederacy.* New York: The Macmillan Co., 1954.

_____. *The Mind of the Old South.* Baton Rouge: Louisiana State University Press, 1964.

Echoes from the South. Comprising the Most Important Speeches, Proclamations, and Public Acts Emanating from the South during the Late War. New York: E. B. Treat & Co., 1866.

Elliot, E. N., *Cotton is King and Pro-Slavery Arguments: Comprising the Writings of Hammond, Harper, Christy, Strongfellow, Hodge, Bledsoe, and Cartwright, on this Important Subject.* Augusta, GA: Pritchard, Abbott & Loomis, 1860.

Escott, Paul D. *After Secession: Jefferson Davis and the Failure of Confederate Nationalism.* Baton Rouge and London: Louisiana State University Press, 1978.

Ellinger, Esther. *Southern War Poetry of the Civil War.* Philadelphia: The Hershey Press, 1918.

Faust, Drew Gilpin. *The Creation of Confederate Nationalism: Ideology and Identity in the Civil War South.* Walter Lynwood Fleming Lectures in Southern History, 1987. Baton Rouge and London: Louisiana State University Press, 1988.

_____. *James Henry Hammond and the Old South: A Design For Mastery.* Southern Biography Series, ed. William J. Cooper, Jr. Baton Rouge and London: Louisiana State University Press, 1982.

_____. *Southern Stories: Slaveholders in Peace and War.* Columbia, MO and London: University of Missouri Press, 1992.

Faust, Drew Gilpin, ed. *The Ideology of Slavery: Proslavery Thought in the Antebellum South, 1830–1860.* Baton Rouge: Louisiana State University Press, 1981.

Featherstonhaugh, G. W. (George William). *Excursion through the Slave States from Washington on the Potomac to the Frontier of Mexico; With Sketches of popular manners and geological Notices.* New York: Harper & Brothers, 1844; reprint, New York: Negro Univ. Press, 1968.

Franklin, John Hope. *A Southern Odyssey: Travelers in the Antebellum North.* Baton Rouge and London: Louisiana State University Press, 1976.

Freehling, William W. *The Road to Disunion: Secessionists at Bay, 1776–1854.* Vol. I. New York and Oxford: Oxford University Press, 1990.

Freeman, Benjamin H. *The Confederate Letters of Benjamin H. Freeman.* Comp. and Ed. Stuart T. Wright. Hicksville, NY: Exposition Press, 1974.

Gallagher, Gary W. *The Confederate War*. Cambridge, Mass. and London: Harvard University Press, 1997.

Genovese, Eugene D. *Roll, Jordan, Roll: The World the Slaves Made*. New York: Vintage Books, 1976.

Greenberg, Kenneth S. *Masters and Statesmen: The Political Culture of American Slavery*. Baltimore and London: The Johns Hopkins Press, 1985.

Grimsley, Mark. *The hard hand of war: Union military policy toward Southern Civilians, 1861–1865*. Cambridge: Cambridge University Press, 1995.

Hall, James E. *The Diary of A Confederate Soldier: James E. Hall*. Ed. Ruth Woods Dayton. n.p., 1961.

Harris, David Golightly. *Piedmont Farmer: The Journals of David Golightly Harris, 1855–1870*. Ed. Philip N. Racine. Knoxville: The University of Tennessee Press, 1990.

Harwell, Richard B. *Confederate Imprints in the University of Georgia Libraries*. Miscellanea Publications. No. 5. Athens, GA: University of Georgia Press, 1964.

Harwell, Richard B., ed., *Confederate Music*. Chapel Hill: University of North Carolina, 1950.

Harwell, Richard. *More Confederate Imprints*. 2 Vols. Virginia State Library Publications No. 4. Richmond: Virginia State Library, 1957.

_____. *The Confederate Reader: How the South Saw the War*. New York: Longmans, Green, and Co., 1957; reprint, New York: Dover Publications, Inc., 1989.

Heyward, Pauline DeCaradeuc. *A Confederate Lady Comes of Age: The Journal of Pauline DeCaradeuc Heyward, 1863–1888*. Ed. Mary D. Robertson. Columbia: University of South Carolina Press, 1992.

Hill, Benjamin H., Jr. *Senator Benjamin H. Hill of Georgia; His Life, Speeches, and Writings*. Atlanta: T. H. P. Bloodworth, 1893.

Hoge, John Milton. *A Journal By John Milton Hoge: 1862–5; Containing some of the Most Particular Incidents that Occurred During his Enlistment as a Soldier in the Confederate Army*. Cincinnati: Mary Bruce Hoge, 1961.

Hundley, Daniel R. *Social Relations in our Southern States*. Ed. and Introduction by William J. Cooper, Jr. Baton Rouge and London: Louisiana State University Press, 1979.

Jones, J. B. (John Beauchamp) *A Rebel War Clerk's Diary at the Confederate States Capital*. 2 Vols. Ed. and Introduction and Historical

Notes by Howard Swiggett. New York: Old Hickory Bookshop, 1935.

Kennedy, George A. *Classical Rhetoric and Its Christian and Secular Tradition from Ancient to Modern Times.* Chapel Hill: University of North Carolina Press, 1980.

Kennedy, John Pendleton. *Swallow Barn; or, A Sojourn in the Old Dominion.* The Library of Southern Civilization. Ed. Lewis P. Simpson. Rev. ed. New York: G. P. Putnam & Company, 1853; reprint, Baton Rouge and London: Louisiana State University Press, 1986.

Lewis, Lieutenant Richard. *Camp Life of a Confederate Boy, of Bratton's Brigade, Longstreet's Corps, C. S. A.: Letters Written by Lieut. Richard Lewis, of Walker's Regiment, to his Mother, during the War: Facts and Inspirations of Camp Life, Marches, Etc.* Charleston: The News and Courier Book Presses, 1883; reprint, Garthersburg, MD: The Butternut Press, n. d.

Linderman, Gerald F. *Embattled Courage: The Experience of Combat in the American Civil War.* New York: The Free Press, A Division of Macmillan, Inc., 1987.

Mason, Sara Elizabeth, comp. *Confederate Imprints in the University of Alabama Library.* Assisted by Lucile Crutcher and Sarah A. Verner. With a foreword by Wm. Stanley Hoole. University, AL: n.p., 1961.

Massey, Mary Elizabeth. *Ersatz in the Confederacy.* Columbia: University of South Carolina Press, 1952.

Mayes, Edward. *Lucius Q. C. Lamar: His Life, Times, and Speeches, 1825–1893.* 2d ed. Nashville: Publishing House of the Methodist Episcopal Church South. Barbee and Smith, Agents, 1896.

McCaffrey, James M. *Army of Manifest Destiny: The American Soldier in the Mexican War, 1846–1848.* The American Social Experience Series, No. 23. New York and London: New York University Press, 1992.

McKitrick, Eric L., ed. *Slavery Defended: The Views of the Old South.* Englewood Cliffs, NJ: A Spectrum Book published by Prentice-Hall, Inc., 1963.

Merchant, John Holt. "Laurence M. Keitt: South Carolina Fire Eater." Ph.D. diss., University of Virginia, 1976.

Mohr, Clarence L. *On the Threshold of Freedom: Masters and Slaves in Civil War Georgia.* Athens and London: University of Georgia Press, 1986.

Moore, Frank, ed., *The Rebellion Record: A Diary of American Events, with Documents, Narratives, Illustrative Incidents, Poetry, etc.* 12 Vols. New York: D. Van Nostrand: 1864–1868.

Nisbet, James Cooper. *Four Years on the Firing Line.* Ed. Bell Irvin Wiley.

Jackson, TN: McCowat-Mercer Press, Inc. 1963; reprint, Wilmington, NC: Broadfoots Publishing Co., 1987.

Norton, Anne. *Alternative Americas: A Reading of Antebellum Political Culture.* Chicago and London: University of Chicago Press, 1986.

Norton, Herman. *Rebel Religion: The Story of Confederate Chaplains.* St. Louis: The Bethany Press, 1961.

Nugent, William L. *My Dear Nellie: The Civil War Letters of William L. Nugent to Eleanor Smith Nugent.* Eds. William M. Cash and Lucy Somerville Howorth. Jackson: University Press of Mississippi, 1977.

Paludan, Phillip Shaw. *Victims: A True Story of the Civil War.* Knoxville: The University of Tennessee Press, 1981.

Parrish, T. Michael, Robert M. Willingham, Jr. *Confederate Imprints: A Bibliography of Southern Publications from Secession to Surrender (Expanding and Revising the Earlier Works of Marjorie Crandall and Richard Harwell).* Austin, TX: Jenkins Publishing Co., 1987.

Pember, Phoebe Yates. *A Southern Woman's Story; Life in Confederate Richmond. Including unpublished letters Written from the Chimborazo Hospital.* Ed. by Bell Irvin Wiley. Jackson, TN: McCowat-Mercer Press, Inc. 1959.

Peticolas, A. B. *Rebels on the Rio Grande: The Civil War Journal of A. B. Peticolas.* Ed. Don E. Alberts. Albuquerque: University of New Mexico Press, 1984.

"Proceedings of the Confederate Congress" (title varies). *Southern Historical Society Papers* 44–54. Richmond: The Virginia Historical Society, 1923–1959.

Rable, George C. *The Confederate Republic: A Revolution Against Politics.* Civil War America Series. Ed. Gary W. Gallagher. Chapel Hill and London: The University of North Carolina Press, 1994.

Ramsdell, Charles W. *Behind the Lines in the Southern Confederacy.* Ed. Wendell H. Stephenson. Baton Rouge: Louisiana State University Press, 1944; reprint, New York: Greenwood Press Publisher, 1969.

Ridgely, J. V. *Nineteenth-Century Southern Literature.* New Perspectives on the South. Charles P. Roland, General Editor. Lexington: The University Press of Kentucky, 1980.

Roark, James L. *Masters Without Slaves: Southern Planters in the Civil War and Reconstruction.* New York: W. W. Norton & Company, 1977.

Robertson, James I., Jr., *Soldiers Blue and Gray.* American Military History Series. Ed. Thomas L. Connelly. Columbia: University of South Carolina Press, Warner Books Edition, 1988.

Royster, Charles. *A Revolutionary People at War: The Continental Army*

and America Character, 1775–1783. Chapel Hill: The University of North
Carolina Press, 1979; reprint, New York and London: W. W. Norton &
Company, 1981.

_____. *The Destructive War: William Tecumseh Sherman, Stonewall
Jackson and the Americans.* New York: Alfred A. Knopf, Inc., 1991; New
York: Vintage Civil War Library, Vintage Books, 1993.

Rubin, Louis, Jr., Gen. Ed. et. al., eds. *The History of Southern Literature.*
Baton Rouge and London: Louisiana State University Press, 1985.

Ryan, Halford, ed. *U.S. Presidents as Orators: A Bio-Critical Sourcebook.*
Westport, CT and London: Greenwood Press, 1995.

Schott, Thomas E. *Alexander H. Stephens of Georgia: A Biography.* Baton
Rouge: Louisiana State University Press, 1988.

Schwaab, Eugene L. ed. With Collaboration of Jacqueline Bull. Foreword
by Thomas D. Clark. *Travels in the Old South Selected from
Periodicals of the Times,* Vol. 1. Lexington: The University Press of
Kentucky, 1973.

Schwab, John Christopher. *The Confederate States of America, 1861–1865:
A Financial and Industrial History of the South During the Civil War.*
Yale Bicentennial Publications. New York: Charles Scribner's Sons,
1913.

Seabury, Caroline. *The Diary of Caroline Seabury: 1854–1863.* Ed. and
Introduction by Suzanne L. Bunkers. Madison: University of
Wisconsin Press, c 1991.

Seymour, William J. *The Civil War Memoirs of Captain William J.
Seymour: Reminiscences of a Louisiana Tiger.* Ed. Terry L. Jones.
Baton Rouge and London: Louisiana State University Press, 1991.

Sheeran, James B. *Confederate Chaplain: A War Journal of Reveren.
James B. Sheeran, C.S.S.R.* 14th Louisiana, C.S.A. Ed. Joseph T. Durkin.
Milwaukee: The Bruce Publishing Co., 1960.

Shi, David E., *Facing Facts: Realism in American Thought and Culture,
1850–1920.* New York and Oxford: Oxford University Press, 1995.

Shirley, Franklin Ray. *Zebulon Vance, Tarheel Spokesman.* Charlotte and
Santa Barbara, NC: McNally and Loftin, Publishers, 1962.

Southern Historical Society Papers. Vol. 44. Richmond: 1923; reprint,
Broadfoot Publishing Company, Morningside Bookshop, 1991.

Southern Historical Society Papers. Vol. 48. Richmond: Southern
Historical Society Offices, Confederate Memorial Institute, 1941;
reprint, Broadfoot Publishing Company, Morningside Bookshop, 1992.

Southern Historical Society Papers. Vol. 51. Ed. by Frank E. Vandiver.
Richmond: The Virginia Historical Society, 1958.

Stampp, Kenneth M., ed. *The Causes of the Civil War.* Touchstone edition. New York: Simon & Schuster, Inc., 1986.

Stirling, James. *Letters from the Slave States.* London: John W. Parker and Son, West Strand, 1857; reprint, New York: Kraus Reprint Co., 1969.

Stowe, Steven M. *Intimacy and Power in the Old South: Ritual in the Lives of the Planters.* New Studies in American Intellectual and Cultural History. Baltimore and London: The Johns Hopkins University Press, 1987.

Tatum, Georgia Lee. *Disloyalty in the Confederacy.* Chapel Hill: The University of North Carolina Press, 1934.

Thomas, Emory M. *The Confederacy as a Revolutionary Experience.* Englewood Cliffs, NJ: Prentice-Hall Inc., 1971.

_____. *The Confederate Nation: 1861–1865.* Illustrated. The New American Nation Series. Ed. Henry Steele Commager and Richard B. Morris. New York and London: Harper & Row Publishers, 1979.

Thompson, William Y. *Robert Toombs of Georgia.* The Southern Biography Series, ed. T. Harry Williams. Baton Rouge: Louisiana State University Press, 1966.

Thorpe, Earl E. *Eros and Freedom in Southern Life and Thought.* No pub., printed in Durham, NC: Seeman Printery, c 1967 E. Endris Thorpe.

Trowbridge, John T. *The Desolate South, 1865–1866: A Picture of the Battlefields and of the Devastated Confederacy.* Ed. Gordon Carroll. New York: Duell, Sloan, and Pearce, c 1956.

Turner, Maxine. *Navy Gray: A Story of the Confederate Navy on the Chattahoochee and Apalachicola Rivers,* Sponsored by the Historic Chattahoochee Commission and the James T. Woodruff, Jr., Confederate Naval Museum. Tuscaloosa and London: University of Alabama Press, 1988.

Wagner, William F. *Letters of William F. Wagner: Confederate Soldier.* Eds. Joe M. Hatley and Linda B. Huffman. Wendell, NC: Broadfoot's Bookmark, c 1983.

Watson, William. *Life in the Confederate Army: Being the Observations and Experiences of an Alien in the South During the American Civil War.* London: Chapman and Hall, 1887. Reprint. Baton Rouge and London: Louisiana State University Press, 1995.

Wiley, Bell Irvin. *Confederate Women.* Contributions in American History, No. 38. Westport, CN: Greenwood Press, 1975.

_____. *The Life of Johnny Reb: The Common Soldier of the Confederacy.* Indianapolis and New York: Bobbs-Merril, 1943.

_____. *The Plain People of the Confederacy.* Walter Lynwood Fleming
Lectures in Southern History, Louisiana State University, 1943. Baton
Rouge: Louisiana State University Press, 1943; reprint, Chicago:
Encounter Paperback, Quadrangle Books, Inc., 1963.

_____. *The Road to Appomattox.* Memphis, TN: Memphis State College
Press, 1956.

_____. *Southern Negroes: 1861–1865.* New Haven: Yale University Press,
1938; reprint, New Haven: Yale University Press, 1965.

Williams, Jack K. *Dueling in the Old South: Vignettes of Social History.*
College Station and London: Texas A&M University Press, 1980.

Woodward, C. Vann, ed. *Mary Chestnut's Civil War.* New Haven and
London: Yale University Press, 1981.

Worley, Ted R., ed. *At Home in Confederate Arkansas: Letters to and
from Pulaski Countians, 1861–1865.* Pulaski County, AK: Pulaski County
Historical Society, 1955.

Wyatt-Brown, Bertram. *Yankee Saints and Southern Sinners.* Baton
Rouge and London: Louisiana State University Press, 1985.

_____. *Southern Honor: Ethics and Behavior in the Old South.* New York
and Oxford: Oxford University Press, 1982.

Yearns, W. Buck, ed. *The Confederate Governors.* Athens, GA: University
of Georgia Press, 1985.

Yearns, Wilfred Buck. *The Confederate Congress.* Athens, GA: University
of Georgia Press, 1960.